THE ALPHA AND THE OMEGA

STEPHANIE GIANNIS

About The Author

Stephanie Giannis was born in Sydney Australia. Her parents are of Greek origin. Stephanie has completed a combined Arts/Law degree at the University of Sydney and she is a registered solicitor.

Stephanie has a double major in Sociology and Modern Greek and she has a keen interest in theatre and the arts. She has an interest in life coaching and she has obtained a Certificate in Life Coaching by Cengage Education.

Stephanie is a Distinguished Member of the International Society of Poets and has had her work published in the books: *"The Tide of Hours"*, *"Enlightened Shadows"* and *"The Best Poems and Poets of 2001"*.

Stephanie is the author of the anthology: *"Fragments of Truth"* and of the motivation book: *"Envision the Vision...You!"*

The author enjoys learning about different people, languages and cultures and she has a passion for teaching, drama, music and travel.

Stephanie believes that all people have an unlimited power within them to follow their dreams and to pursue their individual excellence if they follow the truth...their *soul*.

Published in Australia by Sid Harta Publishers Pty Ltd,
ABN: 34 632 585 203
17 Coleman Parade, GLEN WAVERLEY VIC 3150 Australia
Telephone: +61 3 9560 9920, Facsimile: +61 3 9545 1742
E-mail: author@sidharta.com.au

First published in Australia 2010
This edition published 2019
Copyright © Stephanie Giannis 2010
Proofread by: Jan Gilmartin
Cover design, typesetting: Chameleon Print Design

The right of Stephanie Giannis to be identified as the Author of the Work has been asserted in accordance with the Copyright, Designs and Patents Act 1988.

The information in this book is based on the author's personal experiences and opinions. The publisher specifically disclaims responsibility for any adverse consequences which may result from use of the information contained herein.

All rights reserved. No part of this publication may be reproduced, stored in a retrieval system, or transmitted, in any form or by any means without the prior written permission of the publisher, nor be otherwise circulated in any form of binding or cover other than that in which it is published and without a similar condition being imposed on the subsequent purchaser.

Giannis, Stephanie
The Alpha and The Omega
ISBN: 978-1-921642-73-9
pp162

This book is dedicated to all those who believe that life only ends when a dream never begins.

Keep dreaming and believing.

In faith and gratitude,

Stephanie Giannis

Contents

Prologue 1

Chapter one — The Beginning (Alpha) 5

Chapter two — Footprints 23

Chapter three — Affirmations 41

Chapter four — Self-Mastery 59

Chapter five — The Road to Greatness 77

Chapter six — Diamond Destiny 95

Chapter seven — Contribution 115

Chapter eight — The End (Omega) 133

Prologue

I begin to write this book knowing that life is about keeping true to your inner light. The alpha is the chance to begin and the omega is the legacy you were born to leave behind.

First the dream and then the persistence to see that dream be realised.

I encourage you to dream big and to plan for endless abundance in your life.

When you exhale love and belief into your dreams, you give them the vital power to evolve and touch the lives of countless people.

Delaying your dreams is pressing the pause button on your true potential and your pursuit of excellence.

So what is it you truly desire? When will you start to live the life of your dreams?

As Johann Wolfgang von Goethe said: "*What you can do, or dream you can, begin it: boldness has genius, power and magic in it.*"

If we were born to inspire and be inspired, why wait for happiness to happen? Happiness happens to those who know what they want and who will do what it takes to attain all they desire (provided what they desire is within the laws of humanity).

We were all put on this planet for a reason and discovering what this reason is, is the greatest secret of discovery that we can make. Of course, our mission will not be a secret for long once we contribute our unique talents and stand up for what we believe in. Once our identity and purpose are on clear display for the world to see, we will be working our magic and be in a place of self-comfort.

David Starr Jordan said it beautifully when he said: "*The world stands aside to let anyone pass who knows where he is going.*"

So where are you going? Are you on the path of greatest growth? Are you improving or are you stagnating?

When will your time be? Will you continue to live in the distant past or will you be present in the NOW? Remember the NOW is called the present because it is a gift given to you. Will you accept the gift with gratitude or will you decide that you are unworthy of the gift and return it to its sender?

Remember what we appreciate, appreciates and what we take for granted may be taken from us everlastingly.

So how will you choose to live your life today? Life is indeed about choices and the choices we make determine where we will end up. What empowering decisions will you make today for a better tomorrow? Do you need to let something or someone go? Do you need to change a certain career path and forge forward in a new direction? Do you need to decide that you will be financially savvy from this moment forward? Do you need to pay greater attention to your health?

Whatever decisions you need to make, choose to make them today in the present. Wishing that some genie will appear to make all your wishes come true is only fooling yourself and delaying the splendid life you were destined to live.

Be your own genie. Be your own best friend and learn that great things come to those who believe that they are entitled to greatness.

"Too low they build, who build beneath the stars," said Edward Young.

Are you building or destroying your chances of a beautiful and fulfilled life?

Are you soaring like the eagle or are you crawling like the caterpillar that believes that it will never be a butterfly?

What were you put on this planet to create, feel, share, speak about and experience?

Do you believe that you are special or is life getting you down lately so that now you believe that true happiness will never happen to you?

My friend, take ownership of your life. You are your own boss and never allow anyone else to rob you of your greatness. Dare to shine and fire the opinions of anyone who puts you down or believes that you are anything short of spectacular.

Great people are those who can make even the most vulnerable person feel great, so decide to be a person who believes in the great potential of humankind. Be kind to yourself and others.

As the writer and motivational speaker Zig Ziglar said: "*Live every day as though it's your last. One day you'll get it right!*"

So decide to be happy today. Decide to re-claim your life and be the great person that you were created to become. Remember it all begins with Alpha…

CHAPTER ONE
The Beginning (Alpha)

"A journey of a thousand miles must begin with a single step."

**Lao-Tze (c.604 BC)
(Chinese philosopher and founder of Taoism)**

In the Holy Bible it says: *"In the beginning God created the heaven and the earth. And the earth was without form, and void; and darkness was upon the face of the deep. And the spirit of God moved upon the face of the waters. And God said, Let there be light: and there was light."* (Genesis 1-3)

Whether you believe in God as the creator or not, you must believe that your life started from somewhere. Whatever your beliefs are, you had a beginning and, therefore, you had your "Alpha". Alpha is the first letter of the Greek alphabet and it represents the start or the beginning of what is to follow. Your life is a series of events or phenomena that help shape your character and the impact that you will have on people around you.

Life does have its ups and downs, however knowing that your life began for a reason and not just for a season is fundamental. Drifting through life believing that life is "hard work" or "hell" will keep you in a disempowered state. Your self-talk cannot be underestimated. What you say to yourself on a daily basis has the power to lift or crush you. So what do you say to yourself?

In Victor E. Frankl's book: *"Man's search for meaning"* (1946), he speaks of the power of logo-therapy and how his self-talk kept him alive in the concentration camps of Auschwitz while most others perished. This remarkable and profound book clearly illustrates that our thoughts can liberate or be the death of us. I will elaborate more on Victor E. Frankl's book in chapter four (Self-Mastery).

Think of Mahatma Gandhi and his elevated spirit, even when he was in jail for seven years for his belief in the freedom of the Indian people from British rule.

Think of other mentors or heroes that you may have. By what set of values do they live their life? Do they believe that they have a mission or a purpose? Are they swayed by each wind that comes or are they firm in their resolve?

So if we run with the idea that your life began for a reason, how can you add significant value to your life and the life of others that will have a profound effect on humanity?

Remember, dare to dream big. If you have one life, you better enjoy the party. Otherwise someone else may just come along, crash your party and become the life of your own party.

Helen Keller, the deaf and blind lecturer, writer and scholar, wisely said that: "*Life is either a daring adventure or nothing.*"

Begin to believe that you are capable of what others may think that you are incapable of. Push beyond your own fears and limitations and begin to design your destiny.

Begin to trust that you are a millionaire that just hasn't banked the cheque yet. You are rich and you have all the resources available to you. Tap into your state of empowerment and claim the grandness that awaits you in all areas of your life.

Write down your affirmations (we will concentrate on this subject in greater detail in chapter three) and rekindle the magic that you have lost of late.

Begin to trust your inner voice and guide. In silence and quiet time your "calling" will come to you. Be true to your inner spirit and work towards giving yourself permission to shine.

Eleanor Roosevelt, the first lady of the United States (1933-1945) said that: "*Life was meant to be lived. Curiosity must be kept alive… One must never, for whatever reason, turn his back on life.*"

So be curious like a child. An anonymous writer once wrote that: "*Children FEEL life. They smell it, roll in it, run with it, see it all around them. Feel the world through the eyes of a child.*"

The Russian writer Leo Tolstoy also asserted that: "*The more we live by our intellect, the less we understand the meaning of life.*"

The beauty of life is to begin each day in touch with source which is spirit. Living a robot-like existence will only lead to inner turmoil, heartache and disillusion.

In order to experience true enlightenment we need to take time to begin to understand ourselves and our calling. Taking the first step out to examine our own needs is the Alpha state of self-power.

We will never reach a fulfilled Omega or End state if we live each day following the dictates of others or the path that someone else has chosen for us.

Healing ourselves means taking the time to listen to our bodies and spirit. Constantly punishing our bodies and minds is like whipping a tired horse that is dehydrated and yearns for love and appreciation. It has often been said that whatever we appreciate appreciates. When our bodies and minds are tired all we need to do is give ourselves the respect that we deserve. We need to take the time to listen instead of speak, to pause instead of push.

Being in the Alpha state is being in the state of self-awareness. We can make each day an Alpha state day. The Omega state day should only come when we surrender our spirit and know that our work has been completed on this earth, leaving behind our deeds, our contributions and our good name.

Life as we know it should be a beautiful mosaic of our memories, our efforts and our kind gestures. Remember we grow when we give and a kind word never hurt anyone.

There is a piece of Paradise within each of us – it is just a matter of believing that we deserve Paradise. If we are non-believers, then Paradise will always evade us. We will never be able to experience an elevated spirit because we never took the time to be thankful for our life here on earth. If we do not believe that Paradise exists then this becomes our reality. We live each day hopeless and bitter, blaming others, circumstances and governments for our own sense of misdirection and unhappiness.

Our belief should be that we are responsible for our own happiness and we have the choice to make changes in our life if we are unhappy with the results that we are getting.

Living a meaningful life means writing down clear and defined goals that are time-orientated and ecological. It is important that we assess our values. A life without values that support us will lead to self-sabotage.

Getting to know ourselves and our needs means being in tune with spirit. Tuning is important. Think of instruments. Instruments are tuned in order for the sound to be just right to the ear. Disharmony will result if instruments are not tuned in order to produce the required notes. Cars also require tuning. What would happen if we neglected to take our car to the mechanic when it was producing mechanical or electrical "disharmony"?

Faults unattended to will leave us stranded. Do you want to be stranded in life? Do you want to live your life in a state of helplessness, not knowing who will come around to rescue you or whether they are equipped with the spiritual or emotional know-how to lend a helping hand?

In life, it is imperative that we are equipped with our own strength of character traits that will rescue us in times of tsunamis.

We need to train and practise each and every day in order to improve and grow. Think of elite Olympic and sporting champions. They train with discipline and devotion. They are devoted to training and sculpting their bodies and minds. They become masters of their craft. They train many times a week, every day, in order to break previous unbeatable records and to remain at the peak of their sport.

We can all be masters of our destiny – the challenge is to break free of procrastination, negative self-talk and self-doubt.

The greatest gift that we can give ourselves is the gift of self-belief and then self-actualisation.

If we truly believe in ourselves and our dreams, then we will do everything and anything it takes to make our dreams come true.

We can become all that we imagined that we can be with faith and self-love and understanding.

Life requires a firm resolve and enthusiasm to do the thing that we said we would do, even when the moment we have said it is has long passed. Passion and commitment to our dreams will assist us in our most difficult hour. When the party is over and all the guests have gone home and we are left with the mess and our weary eyes to contend with, then we know that those who succeed in life often do what those who are unsuccessful do not. Often we need to clean up the mess in order to remember that we deserve to celebrate as well.

Remember there is a season to sow and a season to reap. The challenge is time is required in between because we cannot sow and reap in the same season.

We must first plan to get to work and then we will be graced with the rewards. We cannot expect everything and give nothing to begin with. Life will not happen to those who wait. Life happens to those who take charge of their thoughts and act upon them. Rainbows often happen after a storm. It is our belief in ourselves that will carry us through, rain, hail or shine.

Yes, it is often necessary to cry many tears before we become self-aware; before we understand that we can only be true to ourselves because anything other than truth is deception.

What does it matter if we convince the entire world of our self-worth when deep down inside we are feeling untrue to ourselves?

What does it matter that we appear omnipotent when deep down inside we are crumbling?

Why torture ourselves with lies and delusions? Why continue to be unhappy?

Happiness is a choice. We can choose to be happy at any time in our lives. Even when adversity strikes, we can choose to see that there is a lesson that we need to learn that will someday take us to a new level or place in our life.

In choosing happiness over sadness we should also keep in mind that we need to be grateful for Nature's many gifts and blessings.

To highlight this point, allow me to give you an example of an e-mail that I received from a friend the other day. In that e-mail a young woman was very sad because she was blind and unable to see the beauty around her. However, she had a very supportive boyfriend who loved her just the way she was.

She would say to him: "If only I could see you, that would bring me the greatest joy on this Earth."

"We would marry and I would be so happy."

Her boyfriend loved her very deeply and he was sad to see her so unhappy.

One day though a great blessing came to the young lady. She was granted her sight through an eye donor. She was ecstatic and looking forward to seeing her boyfriend now. However, to her utter dismay, when she beheld her boyfriend, she realised that he was blind. He held her gently in his arms and asked her: "Are you happy, my dear, now that you can see? Will you marry me?"

The young woman sighed with deep pain and regret, saying: "I cannot marry you now that I know what it is like to see."

The young man left with a broken heart.

The next day, the young lady found a small note in her mailbox with small but legible letters. It was from her boyfriend who she had decided to leave. It read: "Take care of your eyes my dear. Every time that you look at your eyes in the mirror, know what my eyes looked like before I gave them to you. With deep love always…"

The above sad but gripping story reveals that we need to be grateful for the people who love and support us in seeking out our dreams. When we rise to attain our heart's desires we should keep in mind those who believed in us along the way and helped us get through the many storms in our life. We need to be grateful and thank the Universe for all of our gifts, for when we withhold gratitude, the Universe may take from us what we have taken for granted and instead give what we are unappreciative of to someone else who will value what we have given away with our lack of love and appreciation.

Marcel Proust has a beautiful quote that reads: *"Let us be grateful to people who make us happy; they are the charming gardeners who make our souls blossom."*

We need to be happy in the NOW and be thankful for all that we have.

Deepak Chopra said: *"Healthy people live neither in the past nor in the future. They live in the present, in the now, which gives the now a flavour of eternity because no shadows fall across it."*

Kindness to self and others is also important. As humans we should seek to offer kindness instead of spreading the every day gossip and bad news that is common in society.

The remarkable Mother Teresa said: *"Let no one come to you without leaving better and happier, be the living expression of God's kindness, kindness in your face, kindness in your heart, kindness in your smile."*

The Dalai Lama also spoke of kindness. He said: *"My religion is very simple. My religion is kindness."*

Therefore, life is about the choices we make and these choices determine our destiny.

Eleanor Roosevelt had this to say about life choices: "One's philosophy is not best expressed in words; it is expressed in the choices one makes. In the long run, we shape our lives and we shape ourselves. The process never ends until we die. And the choices we make are ultimately our own responsibility."

Heraclitus also had the following to say about choices: "The soul is dyed the colour of its thoughts. Think only on those things that are in line with your principles and can bear the light of day. The content of your character is your choice. Day by day, what you do is who you become."

The most important thing in life is to be good to ourselves and to be true to the person staring back at us from the mirror. One of my favourite pieces of writing is the poem by Dale Wimbrow titled "The Guy in the Glass" © 1934. It reads:

> "When you get what you want in your struggle for pelf,
> And the world makes you King for a day,
> Then go to the mirror and look at yourself,
> And see what that guy has to say.
> For it isn't your Father, or Mother, or Wife,
> Who judgement upon you must pass.
> The feller whose verdict counts most in life
> Is the guy staring back from the glass.
> He's the feller to please, never mind all the rest,
> For he's with you clear up to the end,
> And you've passed your most dangerous, difficult test
> If the guy in the glass is your friend.

You may be like Jack Horner and "chisel" a plum,
And think you're a wonderful guy,
But the man in the glass says you're only a bum.
You can fool the whole world down the pathway of years,
And get pats on the back as you pass,
But your final reward will be heartache and tears
If you've cheated the guy in the glass."

So, how true are you to the person in the mirror? Are you setting aims that inspire you and challenge you beyond your comfort zone?

As Michelangelo once said: *"The greatest danger for most of us lies not in setting our aims too high and falling short; but in setting our aim too low and achieving our mark."*

How many times have we heard of, or know, people who are very gifted but who, through lack of self-belief or dedication, fall into a mediocre existence, never living out their dreams? The question that you must ask yourself is, do you want a mediocre existence? Do you want to spend the rest of your life wondering: *What if?* Do you want to look back on your time on this planet with regret and self-pity?

Denis Waitley said it perfectly when he said: *"The reason so many individuals fail to achieve their goals in life is that they never really set them in the first place."*

So how clearly defined are your goals?

Do not be afraid of making mistakes along the way of achieving your goals. Life is all about learning and growing. Perception is projection. What may appear like the biggest mistake to someone may be a significant learning lesson to someone else. A valuable lesson that came to shed light on a situation that simply was not working.

Being creative and staying motivated are other keys to attaining dreams.

Anthony Robbins has said that: "*Creativity is created within you, not by your environment.*"

Katherine Mansfield also put it beautifully when she said: "*I want to be all that I am capable of becoming.*"

It is important to reach out to be our best and to push past our own limitations in order to create the life of our dreams.

Be the beautiful soul that you were destined to be. Enjoy the beauty around you and watch your blessings appreciate with the energy of thankfulness that you give out.

"Beauty is truth, truth beauty – that is all ye know on earth, and all ye need to know." – John Keats (1795-1821)

Being true to yourself may be challenging at times and it may be that you will face some opposition in doing what is right by your soul. In the words of Margaret Chase Smith: "*The right way is not always the popular and easy way. Standing for right when it is unpopular is a true test of moral character.*"

If we cast our minds back to some of the greatest leaders and teachers of time, we will realise that they may have faced great opposition on their road to being true to their purpose. Jesus Christ was, and still is, the perfect example of self-truth conquering doubt by the masses. Even from the cross Jesus uttered the profound words:

"Father, forgive them; for they know not what they do." (Luke 23: 34)

To forgive and accept, while staying true to self and our purpose, is a remarkable way to be. Keep your spirit high, even when others yearn to bring you crashing to your knees.

Ralph Waldo Emerson said: *"What lies behind us and what lies before us are tiny matters compared to what lies within us."*

The wise Herodotus also said: *"The destiny of man is in his own soul."*

In speaking about human destiny, it is imperative that we mention thought. Our thoughts are powerful indicators of the direction that we will go in life. Positive thoughts and attitudes create a gravitational pull. Our chances of attracting good health, success and prosperity increase when out thoughts are geared towards abundance.

Allow me to give you an example of the power of thoughts. Recently a friend has been going through a rough patch, feeling as though life for her is not going as she would like. Allow me to call her Chloe (not her real name). Chloe has many reasons to justify why her life is unsatisfying. There are people to blame, events to focus on and past incidents that troubled her. Chloe feels like things are out of her control and that she has entered a period of great self-doubt and disheartenment.

What Chloe will need to accept is that certain things are indeed out of our control. It is the things that are within our control that we should shift our focus on, like the power of our thoughts. We can indeed change our thoughts and ultimately change the patterns that are appearing in our life.

Although these days people seek quick fix solutions to their ailments, as a society we would be better off if people looked within to see what is troubling them. Medicines are often band-aid solutions to the real disease that plagues us.

A change of scenery, good eating and sleeping habits, associations with inspiring people, reading spiritual and motivating books, taking time out to unwind and cherish moments with loved ones can be a cure to our depleted spirit; much more than a drug to numb our senses and pain. Pain, after all, is an indicator of what is going on in our body and this is an extension of what is also going on in our mind. If our thoughts are diseased then our body will follow.

Think about a car. What happens when your car is low in petrol? You will receive a warning signal on your dashboard indicating that your car may soon leave you stranded if you do not stop at a petrol station to fill your car. It is the same with the human body. If we ignore the warning signs that our body indicates, then our body may soon check out on us. If we press on, numbing our body, mind and spirit to our ailments, then we are creating a dangerous situation where we will instigate our own self-destruction.

As Ludwig Wittgenstein said: "*The human body is the best picture of the human soul.*"

Therefore, do what you can to move your body so that you can create a flow of activity in your life. When we feel well physically, we feel better emotionally as well.

Do not underestimate the power of movement. Exercise is a fantastic pursuit and an outlet for stress and worry from the body. Exercise eliminates the toxic build up of negativity that may be affecting us through non-movement during the day. Humans were not created to sit down at a computer all day!

Be conscious of your body and treat it with respect and consideration. In turn, your body will support you for years to come and grant you the vitality that you need to get your tasks done throughout your day.

Instead of thinking about the gym, go there and work out. No one ever worked out a muscle by imagination alone!

As the film director and writer Woody Allen said: "*Eighty percent of success is showing up.*"

It is, therefore, important to be persistent in following one's goals and staying true to your body, mind and soul.

Dare to be original! As the English philosopher John Stuart Mill said: "*All good things which exist are the fruits of originality.*"

In being original, it is also important to keep in mind that optimism is a fundamental ingredient in attaining all of your dreams.

The French writer Albert Camus said: "*In the midst of winter, I finally learned there was in me an invincible summer.*"

Enthusiasm is an important ingredient in attaining what we want out of life. Norman Vincent Peale had this to say about enthusiasm: "*If you are not getting as much from life as you want to, then examine the state of your enthusiasm.*"

Without the desire to be happy at any given moment in time, we can never feel fulfilled because we are always hoping that we will be happy tomorrow instead of in the present moment.

A good example of someone being happy in the present moment is the very talented actor and director Clint Eastwood. After appearing in more than forty films and directing more than thirty, Eastwood believes that he has no particular favourite.

"*I kind of live in the present,*" he says.

It is interesting to note that while other people have clearly retired by the time they are seventy eight years of age and only cast their mind to their past, Clint Eastwood is happy continuing to be true to himself with enthusiasm and joy in the present moment. *God bless him!*

Life is to be enjoyed in the NOW! We only have this moment to embrace because all future moments are not guaranteed.

Begin to live in the present. Do what you do with enthusiasm. If what you are doing is making you sad, change your habits, change your attitude and change your current environment. Do whatever it is you need to do, to live the life of magic and impact that you deserve and desire.

The Roman poet Horace had this to say about embracing the

present: "*Ask not what tomorrow may bring, but count as blessing every day that Fate allows you.*"

Remember that when we speak about beginnings, there is no time like the present to start constructing our dreams. Remember also that what matters most in life is not what other people think of us, but rather what we think about ourselves!

As the German poet, novelist and playwright Johann Wolfgang von Goethe (1749-1832) said: "*Whatever you can do or dream you can, begin it. Boldness has genius, power and magic in it.*"

So begin your dream. Work your magic and trust in your unique and unlimited potential for greatness.

CHAPTER TWO
Footprints

"No pain, no palm; no thorns, no throne; no gall, no glory; no cross, no crown."

William Penn (1644-1718)

The famous and uplifting extract titled: "Footprints" by Margaret Fishback-Powers reads:

> "One night I had a dream...I dreamt I was walking along the beach with God and across the sky flashed scenes from my life.
>
> For each scene I noticed two sets of footprints in the sand, one belonged to me and the other to God. When the last scene of my

life flashed before us, I looked back at the footprints in the sand. I noticed that at times along the path of life there was only one set of footprints.

I also noticed that it happened at the very lowest and saddest times in my life.

This really bothered me and I questioned God about it. "God, You said that once I decided to follow You, You would walk with me all the way but I noticed that during the most troublesome times in my life there is only one set of footprints.

I don't understand why in times when I needed You most, You would leave me."

God replied, "My precious, precious child, I love you and I would never, never leave you during your times of trials and suffering. When you see only one set of footprints, it was then that I carried you."

Keeping the faith, even in trying situations, is the challenge that we face as individuals in this life-time. The true warriors are those who face fear with belief in victory. No great leader ever faced a problem with hope that they would fail.

In life, we are challenged to rise to the occasion and to keep the faith, even when things do not go our way. Knowing that all will be as it was intended to be is the key to internal peace. We do what we can with the best intentions and then we let things be. We let go and we allow the universe to work its magic. Say to yourself: "Everything will be as it was destined for me." Know that you are worthy of the best each and every moment of your life.

Think back on a time when you had to overcome a huge challenge. In that moment, the challenge did seem overwhelming. However, now that you are where you are today, you somehow managed to find a solution or the universe made things fall into place to bring you to your current situation.

Actually you have overcome many obstacles along your path and you have managed to pull through many, many challenging times in the past. Cast your mind back and you will see just how much you have done and how much you have learnt. Look back and you will see your footprints leading you to the NOW. Your footprints are a reminder of the places, the faces and the situations you have encountered in your life. You have impacted the life of many people along the way and your acts of kindness have been appreciated by those who you have shared them with.

Know that you have a beautiful spirit and that each and every day you are capable of greatness. You do not have to be the richest, the wisest, the most well-connected or the most fashionable person. All you need to be is yourself. Leave behind your own footprints in the sand. Don't step over the footprints of others. You will never be happy trying to be someone other than who you are!

When you think of many actors in Hollywood, most have fame, fortune and prestige, however, many end up hooked on narcotics, in endless broken relationships and many die before their time or fade into oblivion, depressed when the lime-light has faded and forgotten them. The reason for their depression and disheartenment may be that they are constantly trying to keep up appearances, yearning for approval and applause and disconnected from spirit and their own sense of integrity and core values. Fame and fortune cannot guarantee peace of mind. Without internal power and poise, external circumstances can leave a person confused, frustrated and disappointed. Disillusionment may follow and when this happens the downward spiral begins. It is like being caught in a whirl pool, struggling to fight against the odds and knowing that you never learnt to swim. When people do not take the time out to re-focus and re-group, they are gearing themselves up for heartache. No amount of money or popularity can prevent a person from crashing when they have not taken the time out to figure out what is meaningful and important in their life.

It is sad to learn about the sudden death of "stars". People who, on paper, appear to have it all and yet are lacking in personal development. Pride may also be a sign to watch out for before a huge fall. When we are proud, we are too caught up being on the roller-coaster instead of realising that we are getting dizzy and that the ride will end soon. Don't get me wrong, roller-coasters are great fun, but it is impossible to constantly be on a high without preparing ourselves for the lows. Some form of balance is required. Great excesses of anything will wear away the body, the spirit and the mind. The Ancient Greeks said: "*Pan metron ariston.*"

This means everything in life should be done in moderation.

We need to learn to simplify our lives and to spend quality time doing things that bring us joy without compromising our peace of mind. Life is joyous for those who are joy-filled. Those who feel like they are fighting their own "inner demons" every day will never experience internal contentment because they are not in harmony with their spirit. "Inner demons" are a sign of past grievances, upsets and a lack of forgiveness of others and of our own self. We cannot begin to be happy if we are holding onto baggage from the past. We need to address our issues promptly and in humbleness. No one is perfect and it is okay to have experienced what we have in the past. Now we have learnt from the past and we are moving forward in forgiveness and self-trust to the greater good of today and into the future. We are now self-aware and will continue to leave our footprints in the sand as a sign that footprints only end when life does and, even then, we can leave behind a legacy for others to respect and admire.

Remember that when you are in a state of chaos or upset, retreat in silence.

If we trace the lives of significant creators, philosophers, musicians and philanthropists, it can be seen that they took time out in order to create a masterpiece, write a book, compose music or deliver a profound speech. When time is spent in tranquillity, focus becomes greater and the human spirit is able to transcend to that higher level of creation.

However, in order to leave footprints in the sand, a person has to know where they are going and for what reason they are going in the direction they are choosing to go in.

In life, there are too many people wandering around aimlessly, begging for others to show them the way. To this day, I am still saddened by the amount of people living in the streets, wandering around without a home or a purpose. I witness people searching frantically through garbage bins hoping to find some form of "treasure". The truth is that if a person believes that they are worthy of the remains of someone else's leftovers, then life will always be second-rate for them. The challenge in life is to rise above despair and hopelessness to a life of courage and joyfulness. The French poet Guillaume Apollinaire wrote: "*Come to the edge, he said. They said: We are afraid. Come to the edge, he said. They came. He pushed them, and they flew…*"

There are many reasons to fly and yet people choose to walk with their eyes downcast counting away their days, months and years. With this type of mental anguish most people die broke, sad, sick and alone, never having had the courage to break free of their own chains.

The truth is that in this day and age, where technology has progressed so rapidly and people have greater opportunities than past generations, people are also suffering greatly. Youth suicide, depression, drugs and infidelity are topics that cannot be overlooked and we are left to wonder why there is so much unhappiness around? A browse through "FAMOUS", "NW", "OK", "WHO" or some other glossy magazine will reveal the constant struggle of "stars" facing incredible battles to stay thin, healthy, famous and adored. The Luna park life of these "stars" soon starts to take its toll on them and careers often wane, hearts are often broken, finances are often lost and integrity goes down the kitchen sink. In the end, many take their lives, lose their minds or elope to a distant place to escape the very limelight that they sought in the first place.

The moral of the story is that footprints can only be left in the sand when people live for a purpose higher than themselves. An ego life of pomp and glamour is the Hollywood ticket to broken dreams.

Humility leads to liberation. Conceit and aloofness lead to internal betrayal.

At the end of the day, a person may be betrayed and get over it altogether. However no person will be able to live wholeheartedly knowing they have betrayed themselves.

This life is too short for games, excuses, mind play and procrastination. Winners walk with their faith in the Lord and sleep knowing that life is working for their greater good.

For no person who walks with an upright heart will fear the evil that may be near or threaten the beauty of their soul.

Believe that your footprints will be deep and continuous, leading you in the direction of splendid dreams, contribution and self-awareness.

Footprints are exactly what they allude to; the prints of your feet that reveal where you have been and where you are going. It is more important to comprehend where you are going rather than concentrating on where you have been because no person can move forward if they are constantly in reverse mode.

Life demands for us to keep on moving forward. Long backward gazes may be detrimental (think of the example from the Bible where this has been the case; the turning into stone of Lot's wife when she gazed back to see the destruction of the city of Sodom and Gomorrah).

Therefore, the point of life is to keep true to oneself by consistent application of forward thinking and progressive behaviour that inspires, accelerates and encourages physical, emotional, mental and spiritual health.

The challenge that we all have in this lifetime is to believe in ourselves no-matter what. Even when others question our capabilities, we need to trust in our spirit and our infinite potential as evolving human beings.

The great basketball player Michael Jordan once said: "*I've missed more than 9,000 shots in my career. I've lost more than 300 games. Twenty-six times I've been trusted to take the game winning shot and missed. I've failed over and over again in my life…and that is why I succeed.*"

The true believers are those who not only dream but who action their dreams. It is not enough to wish that you were happier, healthier, wealthier; it is imperative that you figure out an action plan to live out the life of your dreams.

If you want to leave footprints in the sand, you must first begin by knowing where it is you wish to go. No one achieved anything great without first imprinting in their mind which direction they wanted to go in.

When a person has decided where it is they wish to go, they must then relentlessly pursue their dream. It is the duty of each person that has a dream to breathe life into that dream or else a dream may perish if it is not externalised.

Life calls for people who are brave and action-orientated. Those who timidly pursue their life's dreams receive timid results that are always unsatisfying and mediocre.

To walk the walk of the brave and to leave behind a legacy is to leave behind footprints that no wind will ever be able to erase with time. The true leaders and believers who have walked on this earth left behind life-long legacies that are unshaken and remembered.

True genius is the ability to rise above the doubt of others and to allow your light to shine. This should be done by example rather than through words.

A person cannot serve two masters at once. The master that a person must first serve is the truth of soul. The truth of soul may be related to God, the universe or the religion of one's choosing. To be true to one's self is one of the greatest challenges in this life-time. No person has greater single power than the person who knows themself.

What is the meaning of life if one does not follow one's heart? What is the ultimate price that a person pays for self deception?

In our day and age, technology has progressed at such a rapid pace and yet depression among the nations is at an all time high. What is the reason for this? Is it maybe because people have lost sight of their "calling"?

At the end of the day, each person must be clear about their sense of destiny. What is it that destiny beckons you to do, say or be?

How do you aim to leave behind your footprints? What cause will you give to? Which lives will you choose to impact? What will you learn? How will you grow?

My grandfather was a man of great inspiration. He gave tirelessly to his large family. He worked hard and never complained although the funds were low and the life was hard back then in Greece. He worked the land in a small village and always had a polite word to say to people. Even when he suffered a serious stroke and was bed-ridden for many years, his concern was for his unmarried son. Strangely enough, the nurse that had been employed to look after him was the lady that would become his youngest son's wife after my grandfather's passing. Therefore, even in his death, he managed to bring joy to others despite his own suffering at the end of his life.

I guess being remembered as a person who wants to share and empower others creates a feeling of confidence in others. We never forget the mentors, guides and teachers who have believed in us and blessed us on this journey of life.

Yesterday, the 5th November 2008, Barack Obama was the first African-American person to become the 44th president of the United States. This event created history and highlighted the importance of self-belief and will power in life. People across the globe celebrated and voiced their opinions about human rights and equality and the search for peace and solidarity within and between nations. Newspapers with titles like: "**America Decides**", exposed the public request for a change in personal power and leadership.

Barack Obama created history not by chance or luck but rather through persistent hard work, courage, determination and self-awareness.

Just think about the rapport and impact that Barack Obama created. Two American astronauts orbiting the Earth at an altitude of some 350 km, cast their votes by secure digital transmission because, as one of them expressed: "*Voting is the most important statement Americans can make.*"

Another inspired voter, an African-American security guard, said: "*With the Bush election, it seemed like black people's votes were thrown away. That took me out of it. When I heard about Obama, it inspired me. He wants to change the country, take it in a new direction, and he thinks of everybody.*"

So what would inspire or propel someone to do whatever it takes to accomplish their dream? Who has a dream? Is this person You?

Think back to the profound words of Martin Luther King Jr., at the Lincoln Memorial in Washington D.C, on August 28th 1963: "*I say to you today, my friends, so even though we face the difficulties of today and tomorrow, I still have a dream. It is a dream deeply rooted in the American dream …*"

It is significant to remember that King was arrested and jailed several times while protesting against injustice and discrimination. From a Birmingham jail, he wrote: "*Injustice anywhere is a threat to justice everywhere.*"

Sadly as it is known, while organising the Poor People's Campaign, King went to Memphis, Tenn., to support a strike of black garbage men. There, on the 4th April 1968, he was shot and killed. James Earl Ray, an escaped convict, pleaded guilty to the crime in March 1969 and he was sentenced to 99 years in jail.

On King's tombstone are the words: "*Free at last, free at last, thank God Almighty, I'm free at last.*"

King's assassination produced shock, anger and sadness. Blacks rioted in more than a hundred cities. As a result, it was not surprising that a few months later Congress passed the **Civil Rights Act of 1968**, which prohibited racial discrimination in the sale and rental of most housing in the nation.

It is imperative to note that Martin Luther King Jr. left his footprints, not only in history but on this earth. His quest for human compassion, truth and equality was no accident. It is no wonder that in 1963, Congress passed a federal holiday honouring King which is celebrated on the third Monday in January.

Think now of your own life; what is it that you can do to create a difference? What unique gifts/talents do you have that you can share with the world and leave behind your footprints?

How will you build on your learning? Who do you need to forgive or what do you need to let go of?

What more do you need to accomplish to spread your message or to live by example?

Who have you inspired by being true to yourself?

In speaking about being true to oneself, it is important to consider our values. What values do we hold true to? How do we see the world and how do we treat others?

Our values are the foundations of our existence, so our actions often mirror the values that we believe in. When a person does something that is in conflict with their values, then inner turmoil results. For example, if someone steals, lies or commits adultery when their values are integrity, truth and honour, then this person will soon find themselves at odds with themselves. Of course, no one is perfect but the more we go against our values, the more out of sync we become with Spirit.

The English racing driver Stirling Moss once said: "*It has taken me thirty-three years and a bang on the head to get my values right.*"

Alexander Pope, the English poet, also said: "*A man should never be ashamed to own that he has been wrong, which is but saying, in other words, that he is wiser today than he was yesterday.*"

Therefore, life offers us every opportunity to undo what we have done, to start afresh and to re-examine our attitudes and behaviours towards ourselves and towards others. This ability to undo should give us enormous strength and will power to re-group and refocus, to forgive ourselves and to seek forgiveness from those whom we have erred against.

God or Spirit is within and around us. If you doubt this, think of a time when everything was going wrong for you. Out of nowhere, someone or something happened to cheer you up. A friend called you to see how you are going. You were invited to someone's party or you received a helping hand from a stranger.

I remember this one time that I went to take out some money from an ATM. The ATM was playing up and it chewed up my card. I was disappointed because I was off to work and this would mean that I would be late now because I would have to go to my bank to sort out the card issue. All of a sudden out of nowhere it seemed, a stranger took out his mobile and offered it to me saying: "*Miss, you can use my mobile if you would like to call your bank …*"

The truth is I had a mobile, so I did not require the mobile offered, but I thanked the gentleman who had gone out of his way to be of service. The stranger left and I took a deep breath thankful that there are good Samaritans out there. Strangely enough, within a few minutes and after thumping the cancel button a couple of times on the ATM machine, my card slowly emerged out of the slot that had taken it.

There is a great movie that I would suggest for anyone interested in the concept of doing "good unto others" as is spoken about in the Bible. This movie is "**Pay it forward**". Without spoiling the movie for those who have not seen it, a young boy is asked by his teacher to come up with an idea that may have an impact and contribute to society. The boy comes up with the "**pay it forward concept**", where you do something special for someone in need but without anticipating anything in return. That person is then instructed to "**pay it forward**" in order to continue the pattern of goodness and inspiration in the world. The movie's message is to show how many lives the boy influences as a result of his good deeds and belief in a better world of giving and hope.

The English historian Thomas Fuller said: "*Great hopes make great men.*" The American motor car manufacturer Henry Ford also said: "*Whether you believe you can do a thing or believe that you can't, you are right.*"

The truth is that our perception of ourselves is a mirror of our projection to the world. What we believe we create and what we run from can often sneak up and find us. Therefore, first and foremost, we need to address any issues that we have within us in order for us to see the world with clear eyes. Often what we believe is missing from our world is often lacking within us. First we need to nurture belief within and then we can externalise this belief outward.

True leaders leave their footprints because they have a firm understanding of self and what their mission is in this lifetime. They do not seek affirmation from observers; they look for affirmation within and then they attract observers far and wide.

Think of all the great leaders you know. What type of character traits do they possess?

A fantastic and inspiring book that I absolutely adore is Paulo Coelho's book: "**The Alchemist**", Harper Perennial edition, © 1998, USA. In this book, a young shepherd boy, Santiago, goes on a journey to find his truth. He encounters many obstacles along the way, as well as a guide, the alchemist, who teaches him about himself and what he must learn in order to become the person that he desires. This is a profound book about self-enlightenment and the spiritual quest for meaning and inner fulfilment. Understanding the nature of self-truth is imperative and this book will speak true to anyone searching for "alchemy" in their lives.

"**The Alchemist**" has been translated into sixty seven languages and holds the Guinness world record for the book translated into the most languages. It has sold over one hundred million copies worldwide and has, therefore, become one of the best-selling books of all time.

The book is very symbolic and speaks about finding the "treasure". As Santiago leaves his home in Spain to go to Egypt to find the "treasure" that he seeks, we learn about the importance of courage and determination to leave one's comfort zone in order to gain wisdom and to discover one's wildest dreams as Santiago does through his journey and encounters.

"**The Alchemist**" suggests that we must listen to our hearts and that no heart suffers when it searches for its dreams. So, what "magic" inspires your soul? "Magic" here means the juice or the essence of life that brings meaning or purpose to your existence. For some, this may be designing houses, for others, it may be contributing to charities, for others, it may be composing music, for others yet, it may be making a difference through the field of politics.

What inspires you? By which means will you create your footprints?

Remember you are a unique and unrepeatable person and you only get one chance at this life time, so follow the magic of your soul. Discover your calling and do everything within your power to claim your destiny!

This life is so precious and short and we must take our lives to the next level in order to experience our own potential. We must dare to get out of our comfort zone in order to soar and to embrace our limitlessness. Everything is possible to the person who searches for their truth. Few follow this path and those few are never forgotten. It is these people who create History, who change fixed ideas and who inspire those who were looking for hope in an often hopeless situation.

It only takes that one person…Why should that person not be you?

Why wait until you are about to take your last breath in order to appreciate that you have lived? Live now for tomorrow may never be…

As Dr. Norman Vincent Peale said: "*The only people that I have ever known to have no problems are in the cemetery.*"

If life presents itself with obstacles, then it is how we respond to our obstacles that makes all the difference. We need to rise above our own ego and accept that to live is to often make decisions that we may be unsatisfied with later. This is all okay as we live and grow as long as we are able to see where we erred in our judgment or actions.

Know that it is okay to be yourself and, as Oscar Wilde said: "*Be yourself. Everyone else is already taken.*"

Also remember that, as Bob Proctor says: "*You are born rich.*" You are rich both internally and externally. Believe that you are a multi-millionaire that just hasn't banked the cheque yet.

Opportunities are present; we just need to believe that this is the case. As the wise Napoleon Hill suggested: "*Don't search for opportunity in the distance but embrace it where you are.*"

Your power of decision making is a fundamental key in living out the life that you always desired. It has been said that successful people make their minds up quickly and then take a very long time to change their mind once they have made a decision. On the contrary unsuccessful people take a very long time to make up their minds and, when they eventually do, they change their minds quickly and repeatedly.

Anthony Robbins has said that: "*Your destiny is shaped in your moments of decision.*"

Decision making can appear daunting, especially when you are unsure if you are making the correct decision at that particular time or in that particular situation. Our emotions may also be involved, as may be another person. We may be deliberating over whether we need to let something or someone go and this may both hurt or confuse us.

At moments when we feel unsure, we should remember to exercise silence. Praying also helps, if you believe in a higher source, be that God or Spirit.

Mother Teresa's prayer is a powerful and helpful one. It reads:

> "*May today there be peace within. May you trust God that you are exactly where you are meant to be. May you not forget the infinite possibilities that are born of faith. May you use those gifts that you received and pass on the love that has been given to you… May you be content knowing you are a child of God… Let this presence settle into your bones and allow your soul the freedom to sing, dance, praise and love. It is there for each and every one of you.*"

Therefore, have faith to pursue your God given talents and to share your insights with others. Ultimately you will find that by giving to others you will in turn give to yourself. You will lead by example and so build a reputation of reliability with your compassion, enthusiasm and comfort in your own skin. Reach out and contribute today…Create your legacy!

Chapter Three
Affirmations

"Those who hope in the Lord will renew their strength. They will soar on wings like eagles; they will run and not grow weary, they will walk and not be faint."

Isaiah (40:31)

What is your self-talk like? What affirmations have you written down? Do you read your affirmations daily?

If the term affirmation is a new one for you, do not fear – it is never too late to begin creating your unique affirmations for yourself. Below is a guide for suggestions on affirmations.

Affirmations are in the present tense. You may begin by saying: I *affirm that*...:

- I am a unique and gifted soul who is improving constantly and leaving behind a legacy;

- I am a money magnet, I am attracting opportunities of growth every single day;

- I am a motivator; a leader of inspiration;

- I have excellent health and I am attracting loving people and situations my way;

- I have all the skills and talents I need to attract abundance in every area of my life;

- I am an enthusiast. I am blessed with love, joy and rare qualities;

- I am living my dreams and I am passionate about the path that I am on;

- I am working for the greater good of humanity and I give everything my best shot;

- I am kind and affectionate. I am giving and understanding. I am sincere and I have faith in the ultimate destiny that awaits me;

- I am a person of integrity. I am making sound choices that are driving me in the direction of my dreams;

- I am punctual and I give each person I meet my undivided attention;

- I am excellent in seeking out opportunities that will help me in my chosen path;

- I am great at time management;

- I know how to manage my savings. I pay myself first;

- I am spiritual and I give thanks for my many blessings daily;

- I am in awe of my own life. I am the director in my own life script;

- I am full of energy and I know what is best for my life;

- I am firm in my resolve. I lead, not follow;

- I take care of my body and I eat in moderation;

- I am investing my time with family and friends who I love and care for;

- I am a great person who has much to offer;

- I look at the positives in life and trust in my inner voice as my guide;

- I am self-aware and in charge of my thoughts and emotions;

- I am enriching the lives of those around me and people see me as a life inspired soul;

- I am attracting my goals into my life through hard work and intuition;

- I am my own best friend and I am self-sufficient and self-reliant;

- I am growing constantly and I am a sponge that soaks in valuable information for my extraordinary life;

- I am deserving of all the best in love and I love my life, while I respect the life of other people;

- I am motivated and I motivate others who choose to reach for their unique dreams also;

- I have an adventurous spirit that loves creative pursuits;

- I am an unrepeatable person who creates magic in my own life and in the life of others;

- My life's purpose is to give great love and to experience many beautiful memories of laughter and togetherness with someone sincere and kind;

- I deserve the best of everything in life because I am being the best person that I can be.

Affirmations are the jewels that adorn our inner kingdom of hope and insight.

By writing down our affirmations, we re-enforce our mission statements, desires, goals and self-worth. We give our existence meaning and our spirit realises that it has wings to fly.

Personally, I have always been fascinated with eagles. I have collected many images of eagles and I have written a poem on the eagle in my anthology: "*Fragments of Truth*".

Eagles, for me, represent the human spirit that yearns to soar so high. The spirit does have powerful wings like the eagle. It is just that people often doubt that the spirit has wings so they program themselves to believe that they have to walk everywhere and live the life of hardship and struggle.

We can have all we imagined and we can be all that we aspire to. The magic is to think outside of the box that we have placed ourselves in and out into the endless universe that exists, waiting for us to show up and shine.

Life is too short to be unhappy and directing our thoughts in the areas that we choose will lead to both greater self-esteem and self-worth.

Affirmations are our little building blocks for a better future and a clearer direction as to what we desire or aspire to be.

One of my favourite writers is Samuel Johnson. He once said that: "*Our aspirations are our possibilities.*"

Allow your life's ideas to flow and claim your right to excellence over stagnation. As the Roman emperor Marcus Aurelius said: "*We shrink from change; yet is there anything that can come into being without it?* ..."

So, if something displeases you in your life, it is simple change it! Write down what you affirm instead. Write down what you wish to create/see/experience/feel/attain in your life.

For those of you who have read the book "*The Secret*" by Rhonda Byrne, or seen the DVD, then you will understand that whatever you imagine or think, you attract. This may not be happening to you on a conscious level, however, unconsciously you are pulling towards you the experiences and people that you are thinking about.

It is true that what we focus on, we attract as filings to a magnet. Often what we fear, we gravitate towards, and we cannot exactly explain why this is happening to us.

For example, a young lady that I knew, allow me to call her Samantha, subconsciously feared accidents. She was constantly afraid that she would fall, trip, be bumped into, etcetera. It was no surprise then that she was always experiencing some bizarre accident in the strangest ways. She would always get worked up about the accidents and become frustrated that she had not foreseen these accidents from occurring as she was being extra cautious not to get injured in any way.

So, the moral of the story is that we need to accept responsibility for our thoughts and identify what it is about our thoughts that are creating our experiences.

Think about a racing car driver for a moment. If a racing car driver focuses on the wall, what will happen? Yes, s/he will surely crash into the wall. The reason for this is simple. What we focus on, we move towards. The challenge is to look in the direction that we wish to go instead of focusing on where we do not want to end up.

It is for this reason that writing down our affirmations can assist us in gaining greater clarity and insight about the direction that we want our lives to head in. Not writing down our goals and affirmations greatly increases our chances of crashing into miscellaneous "obstacles" that we subconsciously created through our lack of clear focus and direction.

I read this beautiful piece by William Arthur Ward; it says:

> *"Believe while others are doubting.*
> *Plan while others are playing.*
> *Study while others are sleeping.*
> *Decide while others are delaying.*
> *Prepare while others are day dreaming.*
> *Begin while others are procrastinating.*
> *Work while others are wishing.*
> *Save while others are wasting.*
> *Listen while others are talking.*
> *Smile while others are frowning.*
> *Commend while others are criticising.*
> *Persist while others are quitting."*

Treat yourself with kindness. Know that you are exactly where you are supposed to be. Be determined to change the course of your life around if you are unhappy.

The truth is that no-one can give us what we really need. People can assist us in expressing ourselves but ultimately we are who we are. We live to laugh and experience love and joy, however, no-one can be us because we are one of a kind. No-one can get us to the next level because we need to want to get there on our own.

Oscar Wilde once said: "*To live is the rarest thing in the world. Most people exist, that is all.*"

Life is there to be lived. We need to enjoy the moments that inspire our soul and allow us to share our creativity and joy.

Inspiration can come in both working on ourselves and by also spreading love and hope to others.

In the words of Ruth Smeltzer: "*You have not lived a perfect day, even though you have earned your money, unless you have done something for someone who will never be able to repay you.*"

When we add value to the lives of others we simultaneously enhance the quality of our own by knowing that we are living not only for self. For what good is it to have the knowledge, the wealth and the status if we cannot live life at a more meaningful scale by helping our fellow humans?

The world's greatest leaders over time have made massive contributions to humanity and it is for this very reason that they became unforgettable.

So, what contribution can you make today to be the unforgettable person that you were destined to be?

Affirm that you will leave behind a legacy. Affirm that you will see and do the things of your heart that make you sing. Persevere and keep true to your dreams and affirmations.

> "When you get into a tight place and everything goes against you, till it seems as though you could not hang on a minute longer, never give up then, for that is just the place and time that the tide will turn."
> – **Harriet Beecher Stowe** (1811-1896), *American author and social reformer*

Be confident in your potential. Aim for greatness because you are great!

Allow me to give you an example of believing in your greatness. Recently a young lady told me the following event that occurred to her. Let me refer to this lady as Sally (not her real name). Sally got out of bed feeling terrible. Her day had not started well. She was feeling ill and everything in her life seemed to be bringing her pressure. Going for a walk to clear her head she was startled by the comment of a complete stranger walking past. He said, looking at her downcast and sad eyes: *"Cheer up, it can't be that bad."*

The reason that this comment startled her was because the person saying it was a homeless person with no assets apart from the little sack that he was carrying on his back. Alternatively, she had a loving marriage, family and friends, a job that she enjoyed and her own home and investments also. It is no wonder that the homeless person's comment astounded her. Someone with far less was trying to brighten her day…

The wise Sir Winston Churchill had this witty statement to make about facing a rough stage in life: "*If you are going through hell, keep going.*"

The reality is that life, like the economy has its booms and busts and we need to accept that tough times may come. The challenge is to be a well-equipped sea captain and to keep composed under the threat of the impeding storm.

Life teaches that those with a strong will and a resolute purpose cope better than those who throw their hands up at the first sign of an obstacle. The challenge is not to back away from obstacles but rather to become resourceful and to figure out how to jump over the obstacle. Think of a champion high jumper at the Olympics. The athlete will focus on how to clear the bar rather than on the ways in which the bar will fall.

Visualisation techniques are fundamental in attaining the results that we want out of life. Having a clear end result in mind is imperative in getting there to begin with.

In the example of the high jumper, the athlete may visualise him or herself receiving the gold medal and having the crowd cheer with delight as their National Anthem plays over the sound system. Holding a clear image of your result in mind and experiencing the joy and elation of getting there will enable an individual to fast-track their success in life. Never underestimate the power of visualisation in every day life!

Aim to be the best that you can be. Develop the sheer guts to go after your dream, whatever it is. Do not settle for a second-best life. In the words of John F. Kennedy: "*Once you* say you're going to settle for second, that's what happens to you in life, I find."

So what is success in life after all?

The essayist, poet and philosopher, Ralph Waldo Emerson (1803-1882), had this to say about success:

> "What is success?
> To laugh often and much;
> To win the respect of intelligent people and the affection of children;
> To earn the appreciation of honest critics and endure the betrayal of false friends;
> To appreciate beauty;
> To find the best in others;
> To leave the world a bit better, whether by a healthy child, a garden patch or a redeemed social condition;
> To know even one life has breathed easier because you have lived;
> This is to have succeeded."

Believe that you are a success. Believe that you are on a path, evolving and learning each and every day.

Have the patience and the determination to work towards your goals. Do not allow the cobwebs of your own doubts to hinder or slow you down from reaching your target.

Surround yourself with positive people and read inspiring books and listen to uplifting compact discs.

Read your affirmations daily. Trust in your abilities to create the life that you imagine by first obtaining the mind set of a winner. Someone who will do what it takes to get results without complaining that life is unfair, too hard, too fast-paced or simply too complicated.

Affirm that you are a success and that you have much to be grateful for in life.

Affirm that everything is happening as it should because your focus now has become unwavering and you will do whatever it takes to obtain all of your heart's desires.

Remember you must put in the effort first before any results will come your way. You cannot expect results to come if you do not know what your affirmations are and that you have no intention to write them down so as to hold yourself accountable.

A wise Chinese saying indicates that: "*The rain falls on all the fields, but crops grow only in those that have been tilled and sown.*"

Decide how you want your life to turn out. It is in your moment of decision that your destiny is awakened. Take the time out for yourself to get clear on what you want and who you would like to share your contributions with. Decide to hold yourself to the highest standard.

Being idle and half-hearted will never get you to the summit of your dreams.

Affirm that this life is your life and that you are making it outstanding in every way!

Allow not a day to go by without working on your affirmations and dreams.

You have a magnificent mind and your affirmations that are written and clear are propelling you towards your life's purpose. Believe in yourself. Know that there is no time like the present to begin.

Make a pact with yourself that you will never again put yourself down and undermine your sense of worth. You have so much to offer; just look within and listen to your inner guide. Pay attention to that inner voice that knows you so well. Now begin to work like crazy on your dreams. Remember that good luck happens to those who create it. Nothing in life is accidental. We always get or attract what our thinking is focused on.

> "Good luck often has the odour of perspiration about it."
> **– Anonymous**

Commit to being the best that you can be by choosing to play full out without excuses or procrastination.

In life, you are a unique athlete competing in your own tournament. The beauty here is that you make the rules. You decide how hard you train and how committed you will be. You are you own coach and your own best fan. You choose whether you will compete with enthusiasm and determination. You, and only you, decide whether you will go for the gold in your life or whether you will lose your footing even before the race begins.

It is your life, after all, and you choose how you will live it and whether you will affirm the best for yourself as the unique athlete that you really are.

Dare to push yourself to compete with strength and style. Do things "your way", very much like Frank Sinatra sang in the song ("My Way"). The words to this song are powerful and insightful. The last three verses of the song read:

> *"I've loved, I've laughed and cried.*
> *I've had my fill; my share of losing.*
> *And now, as tears subside,*
> *I find it all so amusing.*
> *To think I did all that;*
> *And may I say – not in a shy way,*
> *No, oh no not me,*
> *I did it my way.*
> *For what is a man, what has he got?*
> *If not himself, then he has naught.*
> *To say the words he truly feels;*
> *And not the words of one who kneels.*
> *The record shows I took the blows –*
> *And did it my way!"*

So, will you do things *"your way"*? Will you be game enough to let go of the known and venture out into the unknown to discover your greatest strengths and sense of self and contribution?

What type of self-talk do you engage in? Do you affirm that you are a success creating your legacy? What will "the record" as Sinatra refers to in the song "My Way", show about you?

Believe in your dreams. As Langston Hughes said: "*Hold fast to dreams, for if dreams die, life is a broken winged bird that cannot fly.*"

When you follow your dreams and keep true to your affirmations, the door to happiness will open for you. For as Democritus stated: "*Happiness resides not in possessions and not in gold; the feeling of happiness dwells in the soul.*"

What makes you happy?

What big dreams do you yearn to live out?

In the words of David Burns: "*There is only one person who could ever make you happy, and that person is you.*"

Understand that each day that passes will be a day that can never return. What have you done today to create a difference in your life and in the lives of others?

Have you read your affirmations? Have you added affirmations to your journal or prosperity book?

Yes, we all deserve to give ourselves the gift of a dream book or prosperity journal. If you have not invested in one yet, go out and buy one today. Find a blank journal that catches your eye with an inspiring cover and begin to write out your affirmations in order to create the life that you want. There is nothing more powerful than committing your ideas to paper. If you see it in your mind's eye, then write it down. Ideas that are merely in our mind and have not been put in a concrete form, that is in writing, tend to be procrastinated upon.

Begin to hold yourself accountable and to take ownership of your thoughts and ideas. Your ideas are your key to hitting the real jackpot in your life. You are your own lottery ticket, so go ahead and write down your multi-million dollar ideas!

Marcus Aurelius said with wisdom: *"Such as are thy habitual thoughts, such also will be the character of thy mind; for the soul is dyed by the thoughts."*

In saying that our thoughts shape our destiny it is important to mention that humans are indeed creatures of their habits.

As Aristotle said: *"We are what we repeatedly do. Excellence, therefore, is not an act but a habit."*

If humans are defined by their actions and habits then what is it that you do repeatedly in your life? What do you mostly focus upon?

If you are uncertain of the road ahead or where your destiny lies, then why not go and ask someone who has something in life that you desire? If you are unable to speak to them directly, observe them or watch them on television if they are well-known. What type of character traits does this person possess? How do they deal with others in business or in their personal lives? If we take the example of Donald Trump, what type of work ethic do you think that he possesses?

As the Chinese proverb suggests: *"If you would know the road ahead, ask someone who has travelled it."*

So go ahead and reach out to find out what it is you need in order to get to where you want to get.

Without action and effort, nothing will fall into your lap. True winners create their luck. They do not wait to win the lottery, which is an event based purely on probabilities.

Commit to your dreams today. Do not delay your life's success. You owe it to yourself and all the other people who love you and who you may assist on their own life journey by being the empowered person that you were destined to be.

"Commitment leads to action. Action brings your dreams closer."
– Marcia Wieder

Affirmations are your utensils for creating the magic and unforgettable delicious recipe in your life. Cook up a storm! You are the chef and you control what you would like to create. As you create, so you will eat. Your attention to detail during preparation will indicate what type of rewards you will reap afterwards. If your meal is juicy, your commitment and passion will show. You cannot hide passion because passion yearns to surface in life!

Think of the talented chef Jamie Oliver. What type of passion does he have for cooking? What type of infectious enthusiasm and energy does he add to each of the wonderful dishes that he creates? Imagine having that type of focus and vitality in life! Imagine how your life would be if you were that excited about your goals and dreams?

Winston Churchill said: "*We are still masters of our fate. We are still captains of our souls.*"

So what excites your soul? What magic recipe do you possess that others yearn to learn about? What do you have to offer this world?

Remember you are unique and talented in so many ways. You have so much to offer. The only thing stopping you from achieving all that you desire are your doubts and fears. Know that no one is perfect but desire is the key to life's joy.

In the words of Vince Lombardi: "*Winning isn't everything, but wanting to win is.*"

Develop the desire to go for your dreams. Write down your affirmations and believe them into fruition. Act upon your goals. Develop an untamed curiosity for asking questions of people you admire who have obtained the type of success that you seek in your life.

Trust in your inner magic and believe that you will obtain all that you write that you will. You will pay attention to your recipe and throw your mind and soul into creating your beautiful life.

As the magical Italian movie, directed by and starring Oscar winning Roberto Benigni: "*Life is beautiful*" (La Vita è Bella) (1997) highlights, life is as beautiful as we make it, after all!

Chapter Four
Self-Mastery

"Self-trust is the first secret of success."

**Ralph Waldo Emerson (1803-1882)
(Poet and essayist)**

Oprah Winfrey one of the world's most successful female entrepreneurs, lives by following her passions. She has said: *"I'm a person who lives my life with great passion and I think that comes across on camera. I believe you're here to live your life with passion, otherwise, you're just travelling through the world blindly and there's no point in that."*

Retaining your focus is a key to self-mastery. Oprah Winfrey has achieved significant wealth and prestige because of her intense focus on her goals and creating a difference in this life-time.

Another key to self-mastery is to never give up. Decide to give each day of your life its best shot, regardless of the set-backs you may encounter along the way. Decide to choose in favour of your passions.

So, when will you master the game of your own life? When will you make up your mind that it is okay to live the best life that you can?

I urge you to become a pupil of your own life. Study your life in detail. Plan out what you want more of in life and develop a plan of how you will decide to obtain all of your heart's desires. Remember to write down your short, medium and long term goals and to write these down as if they are happening in the present. For example: It is the 10th July 2010, I have bought a waterfront house in Point Piper and I am looking into my partner's eyes as we are sipping on champagne. I feel great and truly blessed. This is my life.

It is important to have dreams. Life without dreams is hopeless. As Muhammad Ali has said: "*The one without dreams is the one without wings.*"

Dare to live out your dreams. Dare to be different and to aim for a life of abundance in everything you do. Let no person steal your dreams and question your ability to achieve all that you are willing to work towards.

Surround yourself with people who wish to see you fly. Seek out the people, the seminars and the books that will support your dreams on your road to self-mastery. Remember first you need to become a student of growth and learning in order to then master the route for a fulfilled life. With time, patience and persistence you will be on the road of self-enlightenment. This enlightenment will come only when you are ready to be open to the calling of the universe. This in turn means letting go of past hurts, grievances and guilt that may be holding you back from reaching your full potential.

Learn to be both a believer and a doer. Do what you say you will do even when you don't feel like it anymore. When your word becomes your own law of personal commitment, you will give yourself plenty of references that you mean business and that you are willing to do whatever it takes to make your dreams come true.

Be your own best friend and financial coach. If you haven't already done so, buy a budget planner. This will keep you on track of your expenses, income and debts and help give you a clear indication of what you are spending your money on day by day. By taking the time out to get clear on what you earn and what you owe, you will always be one step ahead of those who haven't taken the time out to assess their financial future.

Remember finances are an important sector in your life. Without clear financial goals and outlooks your choices become limited and your money goes to everyone else rather than in your own pocket. A sensible savings plan for emergencies and future dreams will build your confidence, increase your financial worth and propel you in the direction of like-minded thinkers. Why associate with poverty thinkers when you can have a life associating with abundant givers?

At the end of the day, the decision is yours and only you can be the master of your own destiny with the grace of God, Spirit or whatever else you may believe in.

Life was never meant to be perfect, but we can be perfectly happy being imperfect. The beauty of life is to be the person of truth that radiates hope and love into the lives of others.

Believe in the grace of your own spirit. Trust in the power of your own potential. Be kind to yourself.

Know that you are undefined and irreplaceable. You are the most precious and unique entity that exists.

Belief in oneself is paramount because, when all else fails you or crumbles around you, self-faith can lift you from the depths of self-pity. Remember Spirit wants to see you happy. Spirit wants to help you on your path of fulfilment and self-mastery.

Spirit wants to help you reach for your goals. Spirit wants to assist you on your road to greatness. Believe in Spirit. Trust in its magnificence!

Dr. David M. Burns said: "*Aim for success, not perfection. Never give up your right to be wrong, because then you will lose the ability to learn new things and move forward with your life. Remember that fear always lurks behind perfectionism. Confronting your fears and allowing yourself the right to be human can, paradoxically, make you a far happier and more productive person.*"

As Carl Jung also said: "*Nobody, as long as he moves about the chaotic currents of life, is without trouble.*"

The challenge to mastering our life is to master our emotions. The way we respond to situations, our emotional intelligence if you like, has a great deal to do with what outcomes we create. Allow me to give you an example: two people may experience exactly the same situation and yet may choose to respond in completely different ways. Bob may be diagnosed with a heart condition. He may get angry with the doctor and seek another opinion. He may take it out on his wife when he gets home. He may call into work sick the next day because of his worry. He may become a pain to be around, saying that "bad things always happen to good people."

He may die months later because he simply has given up on life.

On the other hand, Fred is diagnosed with a heart condition. He thanks the doctor for saving his life because he will do everything humanly possible to regain his health. He changes his eating habits. He quits smoking. He begins to walk and enjoy the outdoors instead of spending the weekends on the couch watching television. He begins to read books on health and healthy living. He donates money to the Heart Foundation to help others and to raise awareness. He sheds the excess 20 kilos from his body. He begins gardening and thanking his family and friends for their encouragement and support.

Fred lives for another twenty years, well into his eighties.

As Democritus said: "*Everywhere man blames nature and fate, yet his fate is mostly but the echo of his character and passions, his mistakes and weaknesses.*"

The challenge is to claim responsibility for our own responses in life and how we choose to address the things that do not go as planned. How we respond to set backs is imperative because our responses will show the strength of our character.

In order to practise self-mastery, we need to believe that, as Sir Thomas Brown indicated:

> "Life is a pure flame, and we live by an invisible sun within us."

A brilliant story of self-mastery and courage is that of Cliff Young.

In 1983, a man named Cliff Young showed up at the race. The race was the gruelling Sydney to Melbourne (875 kilometres) ultra-marathon held in Australia once a year. The race takes about a week to complete and was entered into by world class athletes, mostly less than thirty years of age, who had trained especially for the event and were sponsored by the large companies like Nike, equipped with leading high performance shoes and outfits.

Cliff was a 61 year old farmer with no sponsors or coaches. He wore overalls and work boots and to everyone's utter shock he was not a spectator but a competitor. He picked up his number and joined the world class athletes to compete in what is considered the world's longest and toughest marathon.

The reporters, curious as to what this old man was doing, asked him: "*Who are you and what are you doing?*"

Cliff responded: "*I'm Cliff Young. I'm from a large ranch where we run sheep outside of Melbourne.*"

They said: "You're really going to run this race?"

Cliff nodded, "Yeah."

"Got any backers?"

"No," Cliff responded.

"Then you can't run."

"Yeah I can", Cliff said. "See, I grew up on a farm where we couldn't afford horses or four wheel drives and the whole time I was growing up – until about four years ago when we finally made some money and got a four wheeler – whenever the storms would roll in, I'd have to go out and round up the sheep. We had 2,000 head, and we have 2,000 acres. Sometimes I would have to run those sheep for two or three days. It took a long time, but I'd catch them. I believe I can run this race; it's only two more days. Five days. I've run sheep for three."

Now the 61 year old potato farmer with no teeth but an iron spirit did not comprehend the frenzy that was happening as the event was televised around Australia and people prayed that this crazy old man would not die during the course of the tough race.

All the other athletes knew that the race took about seven days to complete and in order to pace themselves properly they needed to run for eighteen hours and sleep for six. The thing is that Cliff did not know this!

So, the 61 year old potato farmer, with no sponsorship or specialised training, kept on running throughout the night as the other athletes were sleeping. Therefore, by the last night, he passed all of the world class athletes. Cliff Young, the man who people doubted and mocked because he did not even run properly with his shuffling feet and work boots, not only did not die but he won the race! Also, he broke the race record by nine hours, completing the race in five days, fifteen hours and four minutes. Unaware that he was supposed to sleep during the race, he said that when he was running throughout the race, he imagined that he was chasing sheep and trying to outrun a storm.

Needless to say the nation fell in love with the humble Cliff Young, who, like his name suggested, was young at heart with his passion for living.

To everyone's amazement Cliff did not even know that there was prize money involved for winning the race, so when he was awarded $10,000 he gave it all away. He said, *"There're five other runners still out there doing it tougher than me,"* and he gave them $2000.00 each.

Cliff Young passed away on the 2nd November 2003. He was 81 years of age and he only stopped running in his final years because he suffered a stroke.

The beauty of Cliff Young was that he was such a giving person. Even when people gave him watches because he never had one, he would accept them with grace because he did not want to hurt their feelings, but then he would give them away to a child in need.

He did not understand why he would need a watch because, as he said, he knew when it was daylight, dark or when he was hungry.

The example of Cliff Young like the tale of the hare and the tortoise, teaches us that with perseverance, courage, self-belief and enthusiasm we can overcome even the most unbelievable challenges in life and silence our doubting critics, while leaving behind our legacy!

In regard to making our dreams come true, Paul Valery has the following insight to offer:

> "The best way to make your dreams come true is to wake up."

Therefore, stay true to your destiny. Believe in your inner voice for self-mastery and raise the bar in your own life.

You have been placed on this planet for a reason and what that reason is, is your mission to find. Have faith that your every step is destined to bring you closer to your objectives and that your journey of self-awareness will lead to your enlightenment and fulfilment as a spiritual being.

Discover your inner wisdom and your talents that yearn to surface and leave their mark on humanity.

Trust that your road to mastery will teach not only you a great deal but also the people around you.

The Jewish poet and philosopher, Avicebron Gabirol, had this to say about discovering wisdom in life:

> "In seeking wisdom, the first step is silence, the second listening, the third remembering, the fourth practising, the fifth – teaching others."

The very talented Andrea Bocelli is an excellent example of someone who has mastered his mission in life through self-belief and discipline.

Andrea Bocelli is today one of the world's most successful male solo recording artists. He has sold an astonishing twenty million recordings worldwide.

Having had the privilege to attend his recent concert in Sydney at the entertainment centre, it was touching to watch this unique man even laugh at himself saying after the intermission: "*I decided to change the colour of my jacket to fit in with the change in the colour of the songs*". "*I hope you like it.*"

It was admirable to see a man who cannot see have the ability to spread humour and inspiration to others.

Andrea Bocelli has made the following profound statements:

"*Destiny has a lot to do with it, but so do you. You have to persevere, you have to insist.*"

"*All that counts in life is intention.*"

So, what is your intention in life?

What would you like to master?

In which way would you like to create a difference?

What would truly make you happy?

There is an insightful quote by Margaret Young that I like; it reads:

> "Often people attempt to live their lives backwards: they try to have more things, or more money, in order to do more of what they want so they will be happier. The way it actually works is the reverse. You must first be who you really are, then, do what you need to do, in order to have what you want."

It is interesting to note how many people are actually living in a state of unhappiness and doing absolutely nothing about it.

Allow me to give you an example. Today I was not in my best form. In short, I went to see the doctor for a cough that I had developed over the last few days. To be honest, I have not been to see the doctor for a long time as I prefer to do practical things to get back on track. However, my cough has worsened and so off I went to see the doctor. While waiting in the waiting room for a good two hours (the doctor had many patients to see), I was both educated and entertained by the plethora of characters in the room. Most of them were chatting about their ailments and, interestingly enough, comparing illnesses, while others were retelling their life stories. I struck up a conversation with an elderly woman who was complaining how she wanted to return back to her homeland, Greece, because life for her in Australia had not been what she imagined. When I asked her when she planned to move back to Greece she was taken aback by my question. Her response was that she could never move back there because her children and grandchildren were here and so she needed to stay here for them. Although I could understand her reasoning, a voice in my head was saying: *This lady will never be happy because her happiness depends on pleasing others first.*

Although it is beautiful to care for others and want to see them happy, being unhappy ourselves means playing the role of martyr where we only look out for the interests and well-being of others and neglect our own dreams and passions.

Strangely enough this lady confessed to me that the last time that she went for holidays to Greece her pains disappeared and that she had used her walking stick only occasionally. She felt rejuvenated and even climbed over rocks on many historical sites in Greece, like the Acropolis, which she revisited. Observing this lady in the present, she could hardly move her feet, was leaning on her walking stick and she had a very bad case of the flu.

I looked down at the book that I had brought with me to the doctor's surgery. The number one New York Times Bestseller: "*The Power of Now*", by Eckhart Tolle (Hachette Livre Australia Pty Ltd., © 2004, Australia). I could not help but wonder why people live in the past and never in the moment. Why do people delay or move away from happiness or simply complain but do nothing about their current state?

After seeing the doctor and confessing to her that I had enjoyed my wait, she responded: "*Why?*" I could not help but say that it was interesting to observe, learn and engage in conversation with people waiting to see her. I told her that I was currently working on a book that focuses on the philosophy, ideology and behaviours of people and the reason behind why people do the things they do. I must confess that I caught both her attention and amazement in saying this. She could not help but smile, agreeing that people will use any excuse to justify their state of inertia or unhappiness.

I thanked the doctor for her time and conversation and the script she gave me and left her room. On the way out of the doctor's waiting room, the elderly lady waved goodbye, thanking me for listening to her. I noticed that I had forgotten about my sore throat and that I had learnt much more than I bargained for from my doctor's visit. I smiled back at the elderly lady, wishing her a speedy recovery. I left a little sadder but wiser, knowing that we cannot help others change if they remain accepting of their own state of being. It is not enough to wish that things were different or that we were happy if we do nothing to create change in our lives.

As Henry David Thoreau asserted: "*Things do not change; we change.*"

So my friend, what is it that you need to change to move towards the happiness that you both deserve and long for?

What is one thing that you could do today to engage in your self-mastery?

How can you shift your comfort zone thinking into thinking of high flying?

Think of acrobats on a trapeze in a circus. What are they focusing upon? Are they envisioning any of the many things that can go wrong and result in their fall or are they concentrating on how to nail all of their jumps to the thunderous applause of the crowd?

What if there is no net? Will an acrobat on a trapeze look down fearing the worst or will they keep their spirit and focus high knowing that they are capable, talented and well equipped to handle their much anticipated jumps?

How do you approach life? With fear or focus?

An anonymous writer once wrote:

> "As you make your way through life,
> Let this ever be your goal,
> Keep your eye upon the doughnut
> And not upon the hole."

Life requires a positive outlook and an unrelenting desire to attain goals and dreams, despite hurdles and obstacles that may appear along the way.

A good dose of positive thinking can take us a long way on the path of self-mastery in life. Do not be fooled into believing that your thoughts have no effect on the outcomes of your life. What happens to you has a great deal to do with what it is you believe you deserve and, whether you realise this or not, you are contributing to outcomes in your life daily, whether this is happening on either a conscious or a subconscious level.

Your inner thoughts and energy are attracting your outer reality. So be wary of what you are thinking about or focusing upon.

Benjamin Whichcote, the English philosopher and theologian, said: "It is impossible for a man to be made happy by putting him in a happy place, unless he be first in a happy state."

So, what is your current reality and what are you responsible for doing to create it?

What decisions are you making today that will impact your future and the future lives of others tomorrow?

What do you need to change or address that you have been in denial about?

What research do you need to do to get yourself out of your current comfort zone and to propel yourself forward in new fields of adventure and learning?

In the words of Will Garcia: "*The first step towards change is acceptance. Once you accept yourself, you open the door to change. That's all you have to do. Change is not something you do, it's something you allow.*"

So what do you need to let go of and what do you need to allow into your life in order to experience the true and marvellous life that you are entitled to?

Remember you are the master of your own boat, unless you believe that someone else deserves to be navigating your boat instead. If you believe that you are not capable of being in control of your own life and the choices you make then, my friend, you are handing over your personal power to someone else who is not you and who, for the most part, will make decisions not according to who you are but rather according to their own personal decision-making process.

Take control of your own circumstances. Decide with conviction and belief what you want out of life and determine what it is you need to do to get there.

Trust that you are being guided each and every day of your life and that you will make decisions that will lead you onto the path that you desire. Keep in mind that no-one is perfect and that your hurdles along the way are only stepping stones for growth and empowerment. Your life experiences will make you stronger and wiser to carry on and to claim the destiny that awaits you.

Know that often you may doubt yourself as you journey on your path, however, if you maintain your faith *"with God all things are possible."* (**Mark 10:27**)

In the **Bible – Corinthians 2:5** it reads: *"Your faith should not stand in the wisdom of men, but in the power of God."*

Therefore embrace your talents and uniqueness with humility and an understanding that your faith will be your beacon of light throughout the dark days of your life. For with God there is only one road to self-truth and that road is through knowing Him.

At the core of it all, self-mastery is an appreciation that He is the "**Alpha and the Omega**" and that there are never any true endings because we are all part of a perfect circle; the "O" that is made complete by eternity.

My friend, trust that all that is happening to you right in this moment is happening for a reason, for your own pursuit of meaning in this lifetime. Without meaning, our life becomes a series of events devoid of any purpose and so a human's constant search is to find a meaning to his or her actions. If you have not read Victor E. Frankl's book: "*Man's Search for Meaning*" (1946), I suggest that you do. This book is the perfect example of a talented human struggling to find a meaning to his life, knowing that he may be killed at any moment in the concentration camps of Auschwitz. His thirst for life and continuity makes him survive his ordeal and live to educate and impact people on a great scale for years to come. The book: "*Man's Search for Meaning*", had sold an incredible 10 million copies by 1997 when Victor E. Frankl passed on and was listed as *"one of the ten most influential books ever written"* by the New York Times on the 20th November, 1991.

As Victor E. Frankl writes in his book: "*What man actually needs is not a tensionless state but rather the striving and struggling for some goal worthy of him. What he needs is not the discharge of tension at any cost, but the call of a potential meaning waiting to be fulfilled by him.*" (page 166)

In his book: "*Man's Search for Meaning*", Victor E. Frankl focuses on the importance of logo-therapy; the ability to use words to oneself to overcome one's current state. Thus, self-talk becomes imperative in survival and rising above one's external circumstances.

As Frankl highlights in his book: "*Everything can be taken from a man but…the last of the human freedoms – to choose one's attitude in any given set of circumstances, to choose one's own way.*" (page 104)

Therefore, what attitude will you choose on your road of self-mastery? Will you decide to lift yourself in your moments of struggle or will you allow your spirit to remain crushed by your external circumstances? Only you can decide, so what will your decision be?

Remember you only get one chance to live, so what type of life do you want to be remembered by? Will you create a difference and path a way of self-truth? Will you become conscious of your own responsibility?

In your own search for meaning and self mastery, will you remember the following quote by Victor E. Frankl…? :

> "A man who becomes conscious of the responsibility he bears towards a human being who affectionately waits for him, or to an unfinished work, will never be able to throw away his life. He knows the "why" for his existence, and will be able to bear almost any "how".
> – (**"Man's Search for Meaning"**, page 127)

Chapter Five
The Road to Greatness

"Keep away from people who try to belittle your ambitions. Small people always do that, but the really great make you feel that you, too, can become great."

Mark Twain (1835-1910)
(American writer)

In Robert Frost's famous poem "The Road Not Taken" (1920), he speaks of the importance of staying true to our inner voice and taking the road of greater toil where our rewards will also be greater:

The Road Not Taken

"Two roads diverged in a yellow wood,
And sorry I could not travel both
And be one traveller, long I stood
And looked down one as far as I could
To where it bent in the undergrowth;
Then took the other, as just as fair,
And having perhaps the better claim,
Because it was grassy and wanted wear;
Though as for that the passing there
Had worn them really about the same,
And both that morning equally lay
In leaves no step had trodden black.
Oh, I kept the first for another day!
Yet knowing how way leads on to way,
I doubted if I should ever come back.
I shall be telling this with a sigh
Somewhere ages and ages hence:
Two roads diverged in a wood, and
I took the one less travelled by,
And that has made all the difference."

Therefore, Robert Frost in his above poem urges us to make up our mind, to choose the road of greatness over the road of external satisfaction. The journey that we need to take is an internal one. This journey will be a journey of self-analysis and introspection. We cannot possibly know where we are going, if we have no destination in mind. Allow me to offer a comical example. A man wants to travel overseas so he packs his bags, informs his work, friends and family that he is going away for a while. He goes to the airport and arrives early to check his bags in to beat the queues. Once his turn comes he prepares to lift his luggage to be weighed to meet travelling regulations. The attractive lady behind the counter asks for his passport and his ticket, in order to issue the boarding pass. She asks: "*Sir where are you travelling to?*" He replies: "*Um, I'm not sure. I haven't made my mind up yet…* The lady looks at him in disbelief and says: "*Sir, I need your ticket in order to know which flight you will be boarding*". The man replies softly: "*Maybe I should go where the person behind me is going…What is your opinion?*" – **Stunned silence.**

The above engaging example indicates that we need to have a clear picture in our mind of where we want to end up or we'll go through life asking other people for directions and we may get more lost than ever in the process. Remember most people are clueless when it comes to directions and, as Allan Pease suggests in his entertaining and witty best-selling book: "*Why men lie and women can't read maps*" (Orion Publishing Group, UK, 2001), most people have difficulty in reading maps, let alone give directions to others.

It is a point of concern to know that people will place the opinions of others before looking inside themselves to examine what it is that they truly want out of life. People are often too afraid to venture out and discover their unlimited potential and instead play it small and safe being the second-fiddle to bosses, so-called friends or work associates who really want to take rather than to give back time or encourage creative flair.

So what will it take for you to be the director in your own script? When will you give back more to yourself and invest in your financial wellbeing?

Do you pay yourself first or have you put yourself at the end of your own list?

Allow me to give you an example of a young man that I know. Let's call him Shane for the purposes of this exercise. Shane works very long hours in his current employment. His health is poor and his finances are even worse. He is always broke and asking for money from other work colleagues. The interesting point to note is that Shane is in a supervisory position and his work colleagues earn less than him. However, Shane invests his spare time drinking and partying to excess, to the point where many days he is unable to show up at work. Shane is looking for significance and love, however, he is always complaining that he is tired and unfulfilled.

Where is Shane headed?

The point to be made here is that no-one can give us happiness. Happiness can be shared but no-one can change our life for us and steer us on a different course if we do not have the willingness or acceptance to desire change.

True enlightenment comes when we let go of past grievances, hurts and upsets and embrace our own learning. We cannot go forward if we are stuck in the past holding onto guilt, worry and disease.

The road to greatness means that we are prepared to let go of our ego and ask for forgiveness from ourselves for our own trespasses unto others. It is only when we are prepared to love ourselves that the universe will allow love into our lives. When we are unloving, we attract unloving events, people and situations and we are left confused, not knowing where to turn.

A young woman that I will call Danielle once confided in me that she is unable to find true love in her life. She blames her past partners, her family and her career for her romantic disappointments; however, at no stage has she looked inside herself to see what she may be doing to bring about the results or lack of results in her life.

The lesson that we are urged to learn in this life-time is that of self-acceptance. We must accept that we are responsible for our own sense of happiness. We cannot continue to blame others for choices that we make that are leading us in the wrong direction. So which is the wrong direction you may ask? The answer to this question is the direction that brings us internal pain and chaos. When we feel unsettled inside, this is a sign that we are going against spirit and that spirit is unhappy.

We need to embrace our inner "child" and let go of hesitation and reservation. We need to stop fearing and start believing in ourselves. We need to accept that we have our limitations but, at the same time, that we are limitless in becoming the best person that we can be. We need to proceed with humility, but with faith and confidence, that we deserve the best out of ourselves and that we are capable of having an incredible life should we choose to.

Discipline is the key to achieving all of our dreams. Nelson Mandela said: "*Discipline is the most powerful weapon in the world.*"

On the road to greatness, we must learn to go for our dreams. As Columbus said: "I *am going for it.*"

Do not allow the reservations, doubts and fears of others hold you back from being all that you were born to be and doing all that you were born to do and create.

King Solomon advised: "*Whatever your hand finds, do it with all your might.*"

Remember that what you may think is a small step may actually impact the world significantly. Never underestimate your contribution or talents. The world needs your input and creative flair. The world needs your skills and enthusiasm. Step up and claim your destiny. Your road was always going to be a great one; all you need to do is believe this.

> "*One small step for man, one huge step for mankind.*"
> **– Neil Armstrong**

The road to greatness also means that the internal balance of a person is imperative in leaving behind a legacy. Have you realised that when your internal world is right your external circumstances are also under control?

Leo F. Buscaglia suggested that: "*There are two big forces at work, external and internal. We have very little control over external forces such as tornadoes, earthquakes, floods, disasters, illness and pain. What really matters is the internal force. How do I respond to those disasters? Over that I have complete control.*"

Meryl Streep, the talented actress, once said: "*Don't let your special character and values, the secret that you know and no one else does; the truth – don't let that get swallowed up by the great chewing complacency.*"

Remember keep true to yourself and do not lose sight of your destination. Take full responsibility for your actions in your life.

A good example of someone assuming responsibility for their actions is Donald Trump.

At one time, Donald Trump was $900 million in debt. When reporters came up to him and asked him: "*What happened?*" Donald simply said that he "*took his eye off the ball.*"

Needless to say, Donald recovered his fortune and is today once again at the top of his game because he "*got his eye back on the ball*" as he later indicated.

My friend, what are you doing or not doing to lose sight of your own dreams and goals in life?

How are you sabotaging yourself from your own path of greatness?

Allow me to give you an example. I had a conversation with an elderly gentleman one day and it was obvious that he was unwell. His voice was croaky and he had a deep cough which he confessed he had for ages. Every time the elderly gentleman coughed his wife became irritated. She eventually said in anger: "*I've told him to quit smoking so many times and he never listens.*"

The elderly man seemed somewhat embarrassed by his wife's remark and he responded by saying: "*You should be grateful that you have a husband who is cool even in his old age.*"

Although I do not want to come down hard on smokers, I could not help but feel that this gentleman had formed a habit that he received pleasure in and, despite the pain that he was now in with his throat, he was doing nothing to address his issue because in his mind smoking was simply a form of being *"cool"*.

The challenge for the wife is that she is in denial herself because you can never force someone to change if they do not want this for themselves.

The truth is that if our body is in pain we cannot perform at a peak state because we are falling short of the energy we need to achieve true greatness. Pain caused to the body through our own actions and decisions inhibits the creative flow of the mind, especially when our mind is focused on habits and addictions.

The wise lexicographer, critic and writer Samuel Johnson (1709-1784) said: "*The chains of habit are too weak to be felt until they are too strong to be broken.*"

What is it that you need to break free from? What habits or addictions have taken the reins of your life and are running you to the ground physically, emotionally, financially, spiritually?

Be mindful of what you do on a continuous basis because, being creatures of habit, we may find that habits, once formed, are difficult to break once we have given them roots to develop over time. Habits must then be uprooted and a root requires struggle and effort to be yanked out from the soil once it has formed. Trimming the leaves on the surface will not eliminate the "root cause" of our pain or discomfort.

The challenge is to admit that roots have formed in some area of our life through a habit or habits and that these roots are causing pain or damage in some way. Without this admission and a burning desire for change, real progress will never be made.

Roots are states like fear, insecurity, a feeling of worthlessness or guilt of some sort towards an event or person.

Remember our past does not equal our future. What happened to us in the past does not equate to what will happen to us tomorrow and does in no way indicate our sense of worth. We are all capable and able to change our life if we develop a burning desire to do so and actually apply our desire to life through action.

The Indian spiritual leader Sai Baba urged: "*Awake, arise and stop not until the goal is reached.*"

Therefore, remember what your mission is and why it is you need to rise each morning. If you have a big enough "**WHY**" you will most certainly find out the "**HOW**".

Remember, you have an incredible energy within you that wishes to express itself.

Apply yourself with diligence. Prepare to astound even yourself with your commitment to follow through. As they say: "*put your money where your mouth is*" and do what it is you said you would do, even when the weather changes, the economy slumps or the car breaks down. Sure hiccups may happen along the way that may frustrate you and set you back awhile, however no set-back can be permanent if we do not allow it to be.

No one can prevent you from reaching your summit if you do not give them permission to do so. Remember we are getting exactly what we think we deserve at any given moment in our lives. If we did not think we deserved something, wouldn't we do everything within our power to change our circumstances?

As an anonymous writer once wrote: "*Choice not chance, determines destiny.*"

The American folksinger Joan Baez (1941) also said: "*You don't get to choose how you're going to die, or when. You can decide how you're going to live now.*"

So, how do you choose to live in this moment?

Will you accept that your road will lead you to externalising your greatness?

Allow me to give you an example of two young women who held two very different views of themselves and their "greatness".

The first lady was Lucy (not her real name) and she had attained great education and came from a family that was okay financially. Lucy was an attractive young woman and she had unique skills and talents that many people would comment upon.

The other lady was Beth (not her real name). Beth came from a family that was struggling financially. Beth was of average intelligence and outward appearance, however, she had great charisma and self-belief. She was a battler who would not take "no" for an answer. As a result, Beth attracted a highly paid job, a supportive partner and enjoyed many social pursuits and engagements. On the whole, Beth was a much happier person than Lucy, who constantly complained about her life and its lack of lustre.

From the above example, it can be seen that self-belief and confidence are important ingredients in attracting all that we do in our lives. Our life reflects our thoughts and so it follows that great thoughts and action attract the great rewards of the life that we are after.

To discover the value of ourselves and to believe in this is fundamental to success in life. Also, it is important to remember that our time should be invested wisely in order to maximise our chances of self-knowledge and development.

As Charles Darwin said: "A man who dares waste one hour of time has not discovered the value of life."

To comprehend the importance of what it means to believe in our own sense of worth is a lesson that deserves to be understood. When we accept that our level of confidence is associated to our level of prosperity in life; then we will do all that we can do to build ourselves up instead of knocking ourselves down.

The Roman poet Virgil said: "They can because they think they can."

So what do you think that you can do?

What type of life do you believe that you deserve to live?

What type of contribution do you believe that you can make?

What type of treasures do you believe that you deserve to behold?

In the **Bible** it says at **Matthew 6:21**: *"For where your treasure is there will be your heart also."*

Where is your treasure? Where are your thoughts and focus? What have you done today to plant the seed for a meaningful tomorrow?

Know that your mission is a special one and each person has a duty to understand what this mission is. Some people realise their mission early on; others find it after many years of self search. Either way, it is okay to be in search of self truth. The only important ingredient is to be aware that you have a mission to begin with. There is nothing more disheartening than to hear that people do not believe that they have a mission or purpose in life.

Sometimes things do not appear to be going our way and we feel overwhelmed, questioning ourselves. We have a fear that things may not fall into place or, worse, that they will stuff up and what we wanted just does not eventuate.

Allow me to make a confession. I found this lovely little quote that is enclosed in a beautiful little yellow and green stand. I loved it so much that I bought it and placed it on my night drawer beside my bed. Allow me to share it with you. It reads:

> "Everything Will Fall into Place
> Life is like a giant puzzle.
> Though our futures may not be clear or turn out exactly as we expected, each of us has the strength inside to put the puzzle together – we just have to look for the right pieces.
> It may seem impossible, but keep striving. Life's pieces have a way of falling into place when you least expect it."
> **– Renee M. Brtalik**

I love the above little quote. I look at it each night before I sleep to remind myself that all is as it is and with faith and courage, all will be well. I rest knowing that with action and perseverance all dreams may become realities. This is what I wish for you, my friend, that all of your dreams fall into place, just like the pieces of the puzzle in the above quote.

Know that your learning experiences along your path of greatness will only make your rewards more valuable because, through your life's twists and turns you will grow and mature. You will gain insight and confidence and, above all, self trust.

In living out your mission, you will spread and share your knowledge and this contribution will in turn create your legacy.

In terms of making the most out of our time on this planet, an anonymous writer said it perfectly by saying:

> "Take time to think…it is the source of power.
> Take time to play…it is the secret of perpetual youth.
> Take time to read…it is the fountain of wisdom.
> Take time to pray…it is the greatest power on earth.

> Take time to laugh…it is the music of the soul.
> Take time to give…it is too short a day to be selfish."

Therefore, my friend, as the above quote suggests, take time for you to discover what it is you want and how you wish to spend your time.

Your time invested in worthwhile pursuits for your soul will bring you great happiness. Your life will have purpose and meaning because you will feel fulfilled as a person, making a difference to your own life and the lives of others.

Have the courage to pursue your road wherever it may take you, even if this road that you have selected appears all uphill at first. Your toil will lead you to self-enlightenment and the gratification that you beat the odds to live out your dreams.

In the **Bible** it says: "For a righteous man falls seven times, and rises again." (**Proverbs 24:16**)

Therefore, do not be perturbed by obstacles along your path, rather have the patience and strength to keep on path, even when the going gets tough.

Remember also that an elevated spirit and mind is imperative when travelling along your road. As it says in the **Bible**: "As a man thinks in his heart, so is he." (**Proverbs 23:7**)

My friend, keep your mind focused and razor sharp. Do not be distracted by what others are saying around you or how they are living their lives. Rather look within to discover what it is you are supposed to do in order to remain true to yourself and your mission.

Again in the **Bible** we are reminded: "*For God hath not given us the spirit of fear; but of power and of love and of a sound mind.*" **(2 Timothy 1:7)**

So, remain faithful, trusting that if you are devoted and inspired to complete your unique mission, you will be guided in your quest.

Your road to greatness is your pursuit for meaning in this world. This meaning cannot be extracted from the outside. It is to be located within and externalised. Truth can only be found within because it is here where the spirit is and the spirit has divine roots.

"*And you will know the truth and the truth will make you free.*" **(John 8:32)**

To know what is true for your soul is to liberate yourself from the chains of conformity. Doing what others do, without asking what your soul needs, is going against your own essence. This is bearing in mind that what your soul needs is righteous to yourself, others and the planet. Above all, your soul must be humble, knowing that there is a power above and beyond it that cannot be defined or confined. This power may be God for you or whatever your chosen beliefs are.

For those who believe in God and the **Bible** remember: "*Do not be anxious about anything, but in everything, by prayer and petition, with thanksgiving, present your requests to God.*" **(Philippians 4:6)**

Keep on going until your mission is fulfilled. The final words of Jesus Christ from the cross: "*It is finished!*" **(John 19:30)** indicate a profound mission. In other words, Jesus knew that he had completed His purpose for humanity. He had lived by example through His teachings and miracles and, therefore, He was ready to depart knowing His mission had come full circle and, therefore, He called out to His Father: "*Father, into thy hands I commend my spirit.*" (**Luke 23:46**)

In living out your own mission, "*be the change you want to see in the world*" as **Mahatma Gandhi** suggested.

Also remember, the great mission of inspiring leaders like Nelson Mandela who uttered on the 20th April 1964: "*I am the First Accused*" only to rise up and lead his nation after twenty seven years of captivity. He walked away from the Victor Verster detention centre, outside Cape Town in South Africa, on the 11th February 1990. In being a free man, he uttered on the 2nd May 1994: "*Free at Last*".

Through his suffering and elevated spirit, despite his circumstances, Nelson Mandela became the world's best known political prisoner, voicing his opinion for change and equality for South Africa's black community.

Some of Nelson Mandela's inspiring quotes are:

"*If there are dreams about a beautiful South Africa, there are also roads that lead to their goal. Two of these roads could be named Goodness and Forgiveness.*"

"*I learned that courage was not the absence of fear, but the triumph over it. The brave man is not he who does not feel afraid, but he who conquers that fear.*"

"In my country we go to prison first and then become President."

"The greatest glory in living lies not in never falling, but in rising every time we fall."

"There is no easy walk to freedom anywhere, and many of us will pass through the valley of the shadow of death again and again before we reach the mountaintop of our desires."

Therefore, my friend, stay true to your own mission whatever that may be. See your purpose through until its end and live a life of moral truthfulness to yourself and others. Be a leader and the example of a person of inspiration, not only during smooth tide but more so in times where the tide rises and appears threatening and overwhelming.

On your road to greatness, keep your spirit high and trust that you will live out your purpose. In the words of Franklin D. Roosevelt in his inaugural address on the 4th March 1933: "The only thing we have to fear is fear itself."

Chapter Six
Diamond Destiny

**"Destiny is not a matter of chance;
it is a matter of choice."**

William Jennings Bryan (1860-1925)
(Lawyer and politician)

Although my background is in the legal profession, I have also had the good fortune to work for a diamond company and to assist them in website presentation and sales. Having the opportunity to see dazzling diamonds of enormous value is of great interest and it is fascinating to learn how diamond value is calculated based on a number of factors. The 4Cs, that is colour, clarity, carat weight and cut, are integral components in determining the value of a diamond.

Like a diamond, life also has a number of Cs that are significant. I refer to them as: confidence, calm, consistency and contribution.

When we are confident within ourselves, we attract greater and more promising opportunities in our life. When we are timid and unsure, we attract like-minded people and situations that drain us of our time and energy. Calmness is another quality that we should aim towards. When we are calm we can make better decisions based on logic instead of hasty decisions based on our moods in the moment.

Consistency is another ingredient in attaining great results in life. When we consistently save, for example, we form a habit of doing so and we pay ourselves first instead of last as I have previously mentioned.

Contribution is the final C in the 4C sequence. Without contribution our life is small and empty. When we dream big we have the ability to touch the lives of countless people on a grand scale.

Think of the diamond once again. Diamonds are formed under a great amount of pressure under the earth's surface. In comparison to your hand, diamonds are small and yet they are worth a great deal and are rare. A well cut diamond reflects light in a spectacular fashion and is marvelled for its brilliance. There have been hearts won with diamonds and lives lost over them, however, the majesty and beauty of diamonds remains timeless. Marilyn Monroe sang that *"diamonds are a girl's best friend"* and the popular term *"diamonds are forever"* has been declared over and over throughout time. So what makes diamonds so special? The answer is that no two diamonds are identical. To confirm this, diamonds are often laser inscribed on the girdle with an identification number. The identification number appears on the diamond laboratory's certificate that comes with the certified diamond.

Do you believe that you are like a diamond? Do you realise that there is, and will only ever be, one you that passes from this earth now and forever more?

You are rare and valuable. When will you decide to be cut out for the life of your dreams? Can you handle the pressure to shape your destiny or will you settle on people telling you that you are a cubic only on show because the diamonds are in the safe. You are a diamond and don't allow anyone else to devalue you. You are not a fake or a copy of someone else's life. Your life is unique and you dazzle with confidence and people admire you. Believe that you are precious and people will begin to treat you this way. Radiate with certainty and the universe will grace you with the opportunity to leave behind your legacy.

If you want an abundant and rich life, believe that you deserve it. It is your birth right to be excellent in all that you do and in the way you design your diamond life style.

Begin to plan now for the life that you are entitled to. Nothing happens by chance or circumstance. All is brought to you through the energy and faith that you exude. Think like a millionaire and money will be attracted to you, like bees are attracted to flowers for their pollen.

So you want to be a money magnet? Find out what people who have immense wealth do. Read, attend seminars and discover your inner genius. What can you give that can add immense value to people's lives? What service are people willing to pay a great deal of money for? How can you arrange your finances so that you pay yourself first every time?

Although money is not the solution for all of life's obstacles, it surely makes the ride a whole lot easier. A wise man once said: "I've been poor and I have been rich and I can assure you that I prefer being rich." The question is not the money but rather the opportunities that money can provide. Why shouldn't life be filled with more choices rather than less? Why shouldn't we have the best lifestyle for ourselves and for our loved ones? Why shouldn't we be able to give some of our money away instead of asking others for money because we are strapped for cash and cannot meet our financial obligations?

Having a clever budget each week that supports a solid savings plan will help your confidence grow as you begin to entrust yourself with your own money. Being financially resourceful is an empowering state to be in.

If we look at all the people who have obtained financial mastery, they are in a position to be able to give back to society on a large scale. Examples include, but are not limited to, Oprah Winfrey, Bill Gates, Dick Smith, Anthony Robbins and Warren Buffet.

All of these people are able to give graciously because they have become masters of pursuing their passions, getting paid a whole heap of money for their ideas and for giving back to the universe to preserve their life of fulfilment and self-respect.

Masters in particular may be rare to find, but then again maybe we just aren't looking hard enough…within. Diamonds are rare too, but there are many undiscovered rough diamonds beneath the earth's surface. It's just that no-one has discovered them yet! You too are a rare diamond. The question is, when will you discover your inner genius?

In order to have a meaningful life you need to begin to believe that you are capable and deserving of happiness. True enlightenment will slip through your fingers if you never take the time out to examine what is important to you in life. You will never be a diamond if what you believe inside is that you are a cubic zirconia. To the untrained eye at face value it may be difficult to distinguish between a diamond and a cubic zirconia. However, on careful inspection under a microscope or a loupe (a hand held magnifier), the diamond can be easily distinguished with its facets and natural inclusions.

At the end of the day, the value that you place on your life is your own. Will you decide to live an authentic life or a life that only appears to be valuable?

I urge you to live a meaningful and true life. True to your potential, your inner wealth and your inner magnificence. If you look deep, deep inside you will discover that your Spirit is working hard to make all of your dreams come true. It may just be that you are struggling against Spirit and subconsciously silencing Spirit's voice. The problem with this is that Spirit wants to speak now. By forcing Spirit to delay what it is it wants to say, you may be putting yourself in a position of heart-ache. Denying Spirit means denying that part of you that wants to aim higher and live a more meaningful life.

So what will your destiny be if you are always suppressing your inner truth?

What price will you pay for living a life of mediocrity and denial?

Will you lose your voice or will you claim the freedom of speech and expression that is your birthright?

Remember, passion makes people light up. When people have a passion they have something meaningful to work towards and create. There are many examples of people who, having been diagnosed with a terminal disease, lived much longer than expected because they had a passion or cause driving them. There are many other people, on the contrary, who had less serious ailments but who passed away before their time because they had lost hope in their life and its purpose.

If you think about all the people who are passionate about something, these people move and speak with purpose and conviction. They often have many admirers and "followers". These people speak with passion and vitality, they are glad to be alive and they have come to realise and appreciate the unique role they play on the stage of life.

People of significance are significant because they first believed it within. External reinforcement should never be traded in for internal reinforcement. Everyone may let you down at the end of the day, but if you let yourself down, you may never be able to forgive yourself for your own criminal act. Yes, it is criminal to knowingly destroy your own life! Your sentence will be life imprisonment and, in many cases, the death penalty. The unfortunate thing is that you will be responsible for putting yourself eternally behind bars. You and only you, will snuff out the life source within you.

On the other hand, you hold the key to releasing yourself from your incarcerated state. You have the power to experience freedom and enlightenment. Never wait for anyone to bail you out or to hold the key for you. You, and only you, are responsible for your own destiny. Claim you destiny now and decide to live in a state of liberty and self-worth!

Life is as precious as a diamond. Hold onto your passions and guard your dreams. There are many dream stealers out there. If you are not wary of your time, someone else will come along to take from you what you have placed no value in. If you believe that you are a cubic zirconia, someone else may just come along and convince you that you are just that. The problem is that you are a diamond and you have sold out to the lowest bidder! Never sell your dreams and time to people eager to see you diminish your sense of self-worth!

As Confucius said: "*To see what is right and not do it is want of courage.*"

Life rings true for the courageous. The timid and afraid only live out the dreams of other people.

Life, as we all know, is quite short. We never do know when our time will be up.

In speaking about destiny, I cannot overlook an incident that occurred as recently as last night. With only a few days to go until the New Year 2009, I could not help but thank God for my many blessings. Allow me to explain; it was about 10pm last night, I had just finished having a hot chocolate with a dear friend and, in crossing the lights at a busy intersection, a strange feeling overcame me. I looked up at a dark vehicle that had stopped suddenly at the lights.

Moments later, when my friend and I had gotten safely to the other side, a large bang was heard followed by a piercing scream.

That same car had hit a pedestrian who had begun crossing on the opposite side of the street. The young man, who looked like he was in his early thirties, lay motionless on the concrete. A large shocked crowd gathered around him. The ambulance soon arrived, followed by the police who were asking witnesses questions.

My friend and I watched in shock from the opposite side of the street as the ambulance workers attempted to lift the man onto the stretcher. He wasn't moving. They applied a neck brace and the ambulance soon disappeared taking the young man away...

In the morning, I attempted to call the closest hospital that I believed the young man may have been taken to. I just wanted to know if he had survived. Unfortunately, as I had anticipated, without a name no-one could help me with my enquiries over the phone so I never will know what happened to that young man on that night.

What I do know, though, is that we just never know what each day holds or how our destiny may change moments or even seconds away.

This incident confirmed to me that blame cannot change what is. What if the young man hadn't stepped out onto the road at that time? What if the driver had kept a proper look out? At that moment, was the pedestrian light red or green on the opposite side of the street? Was the driver intoxicated or speeding?

So many questions that will remain unanswered for me... However, what I did learn from this incident was that circumstantial questions cannot answer the fundamental and burning question that we will never know and that is: "*When will it be our time to go?*"

My friend, I urge you to live each day as if it was your last being true to yourself. Tell the people you care about that they are loved. Share your time, even when you believe that you are time poor. Remember we all have the same amount of time in a day. No-one is favoured or discriminated against because of their class, religion, sex or ethnicity.

There is a beautiful quote by Ralph Cudworth that I like about love and truth. It reads: "*Truth and love are two of the most powerful things in the world; and when they both go together they cannot easily be withstood.*"

So begin to share your love today. Love yourself and your love will be transmitted to others also. We attract what we are and our thoughts are like magnets that draw to us what we believe we deserve.

Your character says a great deal about you and your beliefs. Your character is your shield and armour in this life. A character that is unwavering in the face of adversity will encounter challenges much better than one that crumbles at the first sign of troubled waters ahead.

Cyrus A. Bartol said: "*Character is a diamond that scratches every other stone.*"

Therefore, allow me to suggest that your character has a great deal to do with your destiny. The two are siblings because, without a resolute character, your destiny will be uncertain too. For if you do not believe in yourself and the direction that you are headed in, why should someone believe in you?

William Shakespeare urged: "*To unpathed waters, undreamed shores.*"

Go where it is you need to go to discover your own calling. Be brave against the tides ahead and charter your vessel with dignity and self-assurance.

Your character is your rudder. You may use your character to stop the creeping doubts that threaten to rob you of your diamond destiny.

Your dreams are your own and you can dream what you wish. Allow no-one to rob you of your dreams and the inspiration that is the air to your sails.

To know what your destiny is, you must first figure out what is in your heart. Being true to oneself is probably one of the greatest challenges that we face today as a society. Trying to please others and denying ourselves of our own dreams can lead to stagnation, frustration and disappointment.

In our society based on results, we are running around trying to fit it all in. The challenge is not to be busy but rather to do meaningful work that brings a sense of purpose to our lives. Remember even ants are busy. The question that you need to ask yourself is: are you really in tune with your destiny or are you just going through day to day motions when your heart is not in it?

We may please bosses, work associates, supervisors and friends, however, if we disappoint ourselves what is the cost of this?

What is the cost of selling ourselves short of realising our own destiny?

How much pain must we inflict on ourselves before we come to heed our own calling?

Allow me to give you an example of a young man who decided to follow his calling.

His name was John (not his real name). He completed a combined Law Degree and graduated with Honours. After having worked as a solicitor for a number of years, he realised that his heart was not in it. He had a passion for travel and teaching and discovering different cultures. He came to understand that he was fascinated by wine making and production and so he left his prestigious law firm and became a distributor of wines in Sydney, conducting seminars and arranging tours for people interested in wine-making and appreciation. He travels to Europe and meets people fascinated with fine wine and cuisine and he earns more money now doing what he loves.

So what do you love to do?

How can you convert what you love into a money making process?

The inventor Thomas Edison once said that:

> "If we did all the things we are capable of doing we would truly astound ourselves."

So what are you delaying to do?

What if you did it? Would it completely blow your mind with excitement?

What risk if you took it would take you closer to your summit?

Allow me to give you an example of fearless living.

Bob (not his real name) aged seventy was diagnosed with cancer and given a few months to live. In being given the prognosis from his doctor, Bob went home and took out a blank sheet of paper and wrote down all the uncompleted things he had yet to do. On his list was sky diving, snorkelling, giving to a charity, going up in a hot air balloon and setting up a scholarship at a University to help gifted but underprivileged students. Bob continued to add to his list and, as day turned to night, Bob realised that he had so much more to do before his time was up.

Bob went to sleep counting his blessings and thanking God for having given him some more time to complete some of his uncompleted dreams.

Sure enough, Bob woke up at the crack of dawn the next day and began putting his ideas into action. Within the space of a few weeks, Bob had fulfilled most of his dreams. He went to sleep that night with a smile on his face and a sense of calm, having worked more on his dreams in the last few weeks than he had in the last few years of his life. There was only one thing left for Bob to do and that was to visit his family and friends.

He sat up with his dear friends, laughing and remembering the good old times. He bought thoughtful gifts for his children and his grandchildren and stayed up to read to his grandson, Bob Junior, who had his name. He thanked them all with his heart without ever saying a word about what ailed him.

Lastly, he visited his beloved Valerie. She had taken her final breath five years earlier but he knew she was still with him even now as he faced this confronting time of his life.

Bob passed away in his sleep the following night. He had completed what he had set out to do and his spirit left his body with ease and no pain. He was a grateful man.

So what uncompleted works do you have?

Remember Bob was fortunate to discover that he had some time left to complete his cycle of life. Some people never get this chance and leave the planet with their music still playing inside them.

What is inside you that seeks to be listened to?

What type of music would you like to leave behind?

What types of prayers would you like to be answered?

The English poet and statesman George Meredith said: "*Who rises from prayer a better man, his prayer is answered.*"

My friend, do not underestimate the power of asking for your dreams. In your own quiet time of contemplation and reflection, ask for what would bring joy to you and your loved ones. Go about your day's duties with gratitude and acceptance that the Universe is supporting you on your quest for self-truth and awareness. Remember to take daily action towards your dreams. There is nothing more dismaying than a person with countless talents and little motivation.

Therefore, stay alert, inspired and grateful. Apply yourself with vigour and zest and sow your field. Be patient and one day you will reap the fruits of your labour through your toil.

The wise writer, diplomat and first lady of the United States, Eleanor Roosevelt, once said: "*I could not, at any age be content to take my place in a corner by the fireside and simply look on. Life was meant to be lived. Curiosity must be kept alive. The fatal thing is the rejection. One must never, for whatever reason, turn his back on life.*"

Are you guilty of having turned your back on life?

Do you give up when the going gets tough in order to follow your dreams?

When you close your eyes at night what dreams do you dream about?

What motivates you to keep the faith, even when the weather out is cold and the bills are rolling in?

What do you feel you must absolutely do before your time is up?

Remember some of us need to venture out to find what it is we seek, but this should only be done after we have first ventured within to ask the important questions from ourselves.

Leaving the job, the relationship or the country may not be the permanent quick fix solution that we are after. We see this in cases where people do one or all of the above and yet they are no happier than they were to begin with. The reason for this is that they have not addressed the root cause of their distress or unhappiness and they are at a loss when they cannot understand why, after they have made the external changes that they have made, they are no better off spiritually, emotionally or mentally.

The answer to the above predicament is that unless we sort out what is going on within us, we will tend to repeat our destructive patterns of self-sabotage that keep us bound to our state of unhappiness. Unless we do an internal process of spring cleaning, we will continue to attract unwanted experiences in our lives. If we do not stop and think of what we wish to attract, and commit this in writing to ourselves through our affirmations, we are destined to have more of the same with slim chances for long term change or joy.

Think again of what type of music you would like to play in your life. What type of music best describes you? Listen carefully and identify the beat of your own heart. What is going on deep down inside you? Have you gone within to do your own spring cleaning?

The English writer Aldous Huxley once said that: "*After silence, that which comes closer to expressing the inexpressible is music.*"

Listen for your music, which is the calling of your own destiny!

Remember hearing and listening are two different concepts. Although they appear to have the same meaning, it is important to note that someone can hear what you say without really listening to what you are talking about.

Therefore, aim to hear and listen at the same time. Both hear and listen to your inner voice.

The problem with modern society is that we are so busy hearing that we do not listen for the true meaning of words which are communicated. Most people are interested in their own "story" and only hear what is being said so they can know when it is their turn to speak.

Dare to be different. Hear and listen to what is being said. Give people your undivided attention when they speak. Do not interrupt someone when they wish to reach out to you. You know your own story and it is a story after all. Your story is only a series of events that happened to you in the past and which you often try to resurrect to justify your own actions or decisions.

Let the past go. If there is something that you need to address in the present that happened in the past, do so quickly and effectively. Do not hold onto past upsets because they will do exactly that, upset you.

Your today is valuable. It is the key to your tomorrow and your destiny is waiting for your attention. If your attention is fixated on the past then your energy is being wasted on moments that are done and gone. It is best to embrace the NOW and leave the past where it is, in the past tense.

Your mind is like a garden. Water it and remove the weeds and it will reward you with dividends like aromatic flowers, fruits or vegetables. The soil in your garden is your inspiration. If your inspiration is poor, your garden's produce will be minimal and sickly looking.

Therefore, be wary of how you are tending to your garden which is your mind. Pull out toxic or poisonous ideas once they first sprout instead of neglecting them and allowing them to cause permanent damage to your garden (your mind) later on.

Also be wary of who you allow into your garden. There are many trespassers out there who wish to trample on your soil and steal the produce of your hard work. Your hard work is, after all, your dreams and desire for change and contribution.

How have you been tending to your garden?

Have you pulled out the weeds?

Have you erected a fence around your garden to protect the hard work of your hands?

Remember you need fertiliser to encourage the healthy growth of your garden. Your fertiliser is your enthusiasm. Without enthusiasm, a garden will perish because enthusiasm produces vitality and vitality is what keeps plants alive.

Have you the enthusiasm required to generate your dreams and goals in life?

Your destiny is a rare diamond. In fact it is a D, flawless diamond, which is the highest colour and clarity given to a diamond. It is just that we believe that our destiny is tinted and full of inclusions and, therefore, we jeopardise our chances of happiness because we believe that we are so much less valuable than what we really are.

What are you afraid of?

What is holding you back from realising your destiny?

Go ahead; have the courage to release your fears in order to liberate your aching heart!

In the words of Aung San Suu Kyi, Burma's democratically elected leader and Nobel Prize Winner:

> "Within a system which denies the existence of basic human rights, fear tends to be the order of the day. Fear of imprisonment, fear of torture, fear of death, fear of losing friends, family, property or means of livelihood, fear of poverty, fear of isolation, fear of failure... Yet even under the most crushing state machinery, courage rises up again and again, for fear is not the natural state of civilised man."

Therefore, release your inner doubts and fears and reach out towards the beauty of your diamond destiny that awaits your instruction and awakening. Your time is now; go ahead and claim it!

Chapter Seven
Contribution

"By his deeds we know a man."

African proverb

In life, we are seldom remembered for the amount of degrees, diplomas or certificates we have, but rather we are remembered for the contribution we make and how we impact the lives of those around us on a daily basis.

Often we trade our soul for the duties of life. In our busy state, we forget to be kind to our companions, friends, neighbours, work colleagues and instead we get caught up in the business of it all. Let us not forget that ants are busy too. The question we need to ask ourselves is, what are we busy doing? Are we aimlessly running from here to there or are we focusing all of our energies on what really matters? What really matters to you?

If you were diagnosed with a life defeating disease and told by the medical experts that you only had a few days to live, what would you do with your time? Would you want to express gratitude to all the people who have touched your life in some special and meaningful way? Would you want to contribute, even at that last turn of your life, to the lives of others?

Without love, life is devoid of meaning. Without communication and interaction with other humans, we live a life of meaninglessness. Think of monks, even though they are not within society at large, they share and contribute on a large scale to the monastery they belong to. They work together for a common and divine purpose and their sense of contribution is great and meaningful. They are not concerned with material things of this earth but rather their focus is on spiritual enlightenment and on the contribution to the monastery and its people who have chosen to live for a mission larger than life itself.

In Ancient Greek mythology there was a king called King Midas. He had it all; wealth, servants, glory, status and yet he wanted something more in order to be truly happy. He prayed to the Gods of Mount Olympus to grant him his special wish. That wish was that everything he touched would turn to gold. The Gods granted his wish and gave him the power of the golden touch. At first, King Midas was overjoyed; he touched furniture – it turned to gold, he touched ornaments – they turned to gold. He was overjoyed. How lucky and rich he now was! The Gods had been kind to him!

In his elevated and ecstatic state, the excited king hurried to open a bottle of his favourite wine. Alas, when he touched the bottle – it turned to gold. He touched some grapes – they too turned to gold. The king was horrified. In disbelief he realised what his special powers now meant. He would not be able to drink or eat. He would perish. He sunk into his kingly chair. He began to cry. His daughter heard his tears of pain and ran to him from her nearby chamber. Alas, when she embraced him, she too turned to gold.

The moral behind the myth of King Midas is that without love and a human purpose everything we touch will bring us grief and sorrow. We can never truly be happy acquiring earthly possessions for ourselves without touching the lives of others with human compassion and insight.

Think of the people who have passed from this planet and left a great impact on humanity. I am certain that whoever has come to your mind has been a person who has impacted the lives of many people in a profound way. Whether this person was a mentor, a life coach, an author, a philanthropist, they somehow helped make the world a better place through their human understanding and ethos.

Contribute with enthusiasm and your karma will be profound. The universe will bring good things your way. This may not be immediate or from the same source that you gave to, but something good will come your way in due course.

Be a doer in life. Learn through actions and input.

As the Greek philosopher Aristotle (384-322 BC) once said: "What we learn to do, we learn by doing."

The admirable Helen Keller also said: "I am only one. But still I am one. I cannot do everything, but still I can do something. I will not refuse to do something I can do."

Know also that each day you have given your best. Sleep at night knowing that you did what you could to make this world a better place. Bless each day for its offerings and then let it go. In the words of Lady Mary Fairfax: "...Believe the day is done. Whether it's been the best day or the worst, it is over, let it go."

Letting go of certain things that are troubling us may bring great calm in our lives. Knowing when it is the time to let things go is imperative in self-healing as holding onto past grievances, hurts and upsets only limits the positive new energy attempting to come into our lives.

Therefore, the first and most important step in helping others is to begin by knowing ourselves and giving great self-love to our own being. We will never be able to successfully contribute to the lives of other people if we are feeling chaos within.

Allow me to give you an example at this point. There was a young woman that I met a while ago. Allow me to use the name Melissa (not her real name).

Melissa was an intelligent and admirable girl. She had dated a few lovely young men, however, each time her relationships ended abruptly. She would feel confused and upset when this would happen and would try to analyse why this had occurred.

The truth is that although all of these men were gifted in their own way, she knew deep down that none of these men were the soul mate that she was seeking. Therefore, try as she would to make things work with these potential suitors, each time something would happen to cause a break-up. The truth is because she was not certain in her heart, life had responded by interrupting her pattern and taking these men away to continue on their own path.

The truth is that energy of doubt brings results that are doubtful. Life requires clarity of vision and thoughts of faith and determination.

Again, we are unable to contribute mentally, emotionally, spiritually and physically to another person if inside we are unsure, afraid and filled with uncertainty.

In all areas of our lives, we need to be present in order to contribute, grow and be the best that we can be.

We need to identify what our dream is in order to attain it and contribute on the scale that we desire.

As Carl Sandburg said: "*Nothing happens unless first a dream.*"

Also, you need to know where you are going. Without a mind map of where you want to end up, you may just end up at a place that you do not wish to be at.

James Allen correctly stated that: "*He who cherishes a beautiful vision, a lofty ideal in his heart, will one day realise it.*"

Eleanor Roosevelt also said: "*The future belongs to those who believe in the beauty of their dreams.*"

When we follow our dreams we stay true to ourselves and, at the same time, we are able to branch out and help others with our knowledge, enthusiasm and passion.

When we choose to inject our enthusiasm, time and resources into a task, mission or person, we show that we believe in the potential of what we are choosing to place our focus upon. It is no accident that where we place our greatest focus in life we tend to attain our greatest results.

Think of world class athletes in the various sports. They excel at their game because of their undivided focus and training to the sport that they are competing in. They have developed the right mind-set and attitude to get up earlier than most of us and train over many long and gruelling hours, many times a week over many years, to be at the pinnacle of their field.

Just imagine if we applied that same type of devotion, dedication and belief to our every day lives? What type of a difference would that make to our health, family, relationships and jobs? Imagine waking up earlier than the rest of the population and working on our dreams and goals? Imagine training our brain to excel in life each and every day, for hours each day, over the many years of our life? What type of life would we lead? What type of person would be become?

The truth is that most people live on the poverty line of existence because of their poor attitude and ingrained habits that they are unwilling to change.

I saw a very good movie recently with Jim Carrey as the protagonist. It was called: "**Yes Man**".

For those who have not seen the movie, I will not spoil it for you other than to say that it is about a man who has a poor attitude towards life. He rejects offers that come his way in many areas of his life because he has fallen into a comfort zone. He is miserable, however, he is not being proactive to change his circumstances. Through an interesting turn of events, he begins to open his mind to possibilities and opportunities by saying "yes". His life begins to change significantly. The challenge he must now face and learn is not to say "yes" all of the time but to say "yes" with confidence when he sees that an opportunity is present for self-development and growth.

The American educator Joan L. Curcio said: "*Courageous risks are life-giving. They help you grow, make you brave and better than you think you are.*"

Dare to be a person of courage. Dare to step out of your box and to venture out to develop your learning. Remember if you do nothing you gain nothing and, as the familiar saying goes: "*Nothing ventured, nothing gained.*"

Extraordinary people are those who convert every obstacle into an opportunity. They lead with courage and self-belief in their dreams and their capabilities.

Think about Bill Gates for a minute. The key that made Bill Gates so incredibly wealthy is his enormous self-belief and his determination to overcome any obstacle to achieve his vision.

It is no accident that Bill Gates topped the Forbes Magazine's

List of billionaires from 1995-2007. His billionaire dollar mindset is the reason for his phenomenal success, prosperity and global influence. Although Bill Gates no longer tops the Forbes Rich List (these days he is more interested in devoting himself to the Bill and Melinda Gates Foundation, which is now the world's largest transparently operated charitable foundation), his contribution to humanity will be forever enduring. Along with Warren Buffet, who signed a deal promising to contribute another US $1.5 billion dollars a year to the Bill and Melinda Gates foundation, Bill Gates is a visionary who kept true to his passion and idea of adding value to other people's lives.

It needs to be mentioned that Bill Gates encountered doubters along the way. He was considered a "nerd" by some and so he had to keep true to himself, even if others could not understand his vision or relate to him. It is in response to those doubters that Bill Gates said: "*Be nice to nerds. Chances are you'll end up working for one.*"

Bill Gates has also emphasised the importance of leaders and the role that reading has played in his life. He stated:

"*As we look ahead into the next century, leaders will be those who empower others.*"

"*I really had a lot of dreams when I was a kid, and I think a great deal of that grew out of the fact that I had a chance to read a lot.*"

Bill Gates is a firm believer of doing the best that you can in life without moaning and groaning about your circumstances. Rather he believes that people need to be proactive and take ownership of their lot in life. Our belief about ourselves can indeed become a self-fulfilling prophecy!

"Life is not fair; get used to it."
– Bill Gates

By remembering the example of Bill Gates, learn to develop the higher edge in your life. Decide that you will not sell yourself short of attaining your dreams. Believe that your visions, with hard work and commitment, will give you the results that you seek. Trust in your inner voice, even when others doubt you and question your dreams.

The Italian actress Sophia Loren has this to say about having faith in yourself: *"Getting ahead in a difficult profession requires avid faith in yourself. You must be able to sustain yourself against staggering blows and unfair reversals."*

Remember all great leaders faced many challenges on their road to greatness. This happened throughout History and it happens today too.

We have all heard of the great boxer Muhammad Ali. Imagine coming out of retirement in 1980 to fight Larry Holmes for the World Boxing Council version of the heavy weight title, only to be defeated by Holmes by a technical knockout. This defeat does not change the fact that Ali still remains a great boxing legend and he knows this. It is not our defeats that define us but rather feeling defeated within ourselves. We will lose some matches in life. The main thing is not to lose the feeling of empowerment within ourselves. No one can rob us of who we are and our accomplishments.

In the case of Ali, no one can rob him of the fact that he became the first heavyweight boxing champion to win the title four times.

It is, therefore, important to concentrate on the big picture rather than defining ourselves by individual events that do not go our way.

Remember the spirit is limitless; it cannot be confined or defined.

Self-discovery is imperative in this life. As the psychiatrist Elisabeth Kubler-Ross said:

"Learn to get in touch with the silence within yourself and know that everything in this life has a purpose."

Believe that we all have a purpose in this life and that we can all create a difference by being who we are.

Develop your belief in yourself because there is nothing like positive thinking to help you along the path when you face your obstacles.

Know that it is natural to encounter obstacles along your path. Accept this and become better and stronger.

The Roman philosopher, dramatist, poet and statesman Seneca said: "Most powerful is he who has control over himself."

The American writer Elaine Maxwell also said: "My will shall shape my future. Whether I fail or succeed shall be no man's doing but my own. I am the force. I can clear any obstacle before me or I can be *lost in the maze. My choice; my responsibility; win or lose, only I hold the key to my destiny."*

Trust in your personal power to realise your dreams. Take ownership of your choices and decisions.

Do not lay blame on others for your own circumstances. Engage in positive self talk and work on improving yourself through education, training or seminars.

In order to contribute to the lives of others, you must first contribute to your own and develop the attitude and character of a leader.

Observe someone that you look up to as an effective leader. What type of attitude, habits, and behaviours does this person possess? How does this person contribute to the lives of others? What is unique about their approach or personality?

What types of skills do you need to brush up on to develop a leader's edge?

Let me give you an example of a young man who wanted to be a great leader. His name was Sam (not his real name). Sam was a gifted young man. The challenge was that Sam did not believe this. He walked and talked with a lack of confidence and self-belief and people picked this up. Because Sam did not believe in his own abilities, others soon began to think that Sam was not motivated or the talented and gifted person that he really was. Sam accepted low pay jobs with bosses who took advantage of his time and energy. Wanting to please everyone else but himself, Sam tolerated conditions that were clearly not in line with his true worth. The result was that Sam was overworked, underpaid and very unhappy.

How do you undermine your own sense of self? Do you allow others to take advantage of your unique talents?

Remember we contribute because we choose to. There is a clear difference between contribution out of our own volition and being taken for a ride by others because of a low sense of self-worth.

So hold your head up high. Elevate your thoughts and do not accept behaviour that diminishes your sense of uniqueness. Contribute because you choose to.

Leaders lead because they have a clear understanding of who they are, what they want out of life, where they are going and how they choose to be treated. Yes, we choose how we wish to be treated because, if someone's behaviour is unacceptable, we politely and firmly tell them so. To allow someone to treat us in a way that is unacceptable is giving out the message to the universe that we believe that we deserve that type of treatment. The universe in turn will respond with giving us more of what we are choosing to accept.

Therefore, next time you are accepting some form of behaviour by others, stop and ask yourself is this the way you want to be treated? If not, take appropriate action to set the standard of what is acceptable behaviour to you.

The writer Norman Vincent Peale (1898-1993) had this to say about attitudes in life: "*Attitudes are more important than facts.*"

What type of attitude do you have?

The truth is that the best type of attitude is an attitude of gratitude. We need to be thankful for our blessings, while at the same time valuing ourselves. By believing that we are valuable, we are more equipped to add value to the life of others because we choose to.

If we have a low sense of self, we cannot possibly contribute on a large scale because we are not confident in our abilities and lack of confidence shows up even when we try to hide this.

Knowing that we are beautiful beams of light that radiate our hopes, talents and unique abilities to the world to see, we must strive to embrace our limitless potential.

We must strive to help ourselves to be the best that we can be.

As the American statesman and scientist Benjamin Franklin said: "*God helps those who help themselves.*"

So aim to work on yourself with humility and diligence and watch your dreams come into fruition.

Remember there is nothing more admirable than a person who produces great results and speaks little about their accomplishments. For the truly great people do not need external applause to get a job done with excellence and integrity.

Think about all of the great and inspiring leaders that you know; how many produce outstanding results and yet little is known of their efforts in the interim? Strangely enough, we learn of their significant contribution after they have accomplished their great breakthroughs or accomplishments.

Strive to be a steady stream that trickles quietly without attracting too much attention to yourself as you work away at your dreams. Keep in mind that works in progress are like libraries; they need quiet to function. The focused mind may become distracted with chaos and noise. Noise is the input of others who may doubt your dreams, abilities and insights.

To contribute effectively and on a large scale, the mind needs time to itself to mould ideas, design plans and to investigate avenues for growth and change.

The mind needs renewal and time away from distractions and predictability.

When the mind seeks to take to the skies of invention, it will wish to let go of the daily noise of the known and to venture out into the vastness of the unknown. The unknown is not defined by the sounds of everyday life because the unknown is searching for the divine music of the soul.

The British writer Matthew Arnold said poignantly: "*Resolve to be thyself; and know that he, who finds himself, loses his misery.*"

Therefore, my friend, strive to find yourself and know that when you do you will also achieve your greatest sense of contribution because you will live no longer for the purpose of proving something to yourself but rather to give of yourself to others.

Dare to be all that you were born to be with insight, grace and compassion for your fellow human beings.

Allow me to give you an example of contribution and giving to others.

There were two men. One was named Jack and the other was named Peter. Peter had been in the hospital for a long time; he had suffered burns to 70% of his body in a house fire and his body was taking a very long time to heal. His bed was positioned near a hospital window but he could not see out of the window as his bed was not facing the window. One day a newcomer was brought to the room that Peter was in. His name was Jack. Jack's bed was positioned facing the window so he had a clear view outside. Jack was a talkative person. He immediately cracked a smile and asked Peter what his name was and how his day was going. Peter was in no mood to chat. In fact, he was angry with this newcomer who had been given the window view and who now wanted to strike up a conversation.

Peter couldn't even be bothered to ask Jack why he had been brought into this recovery room, which was intended for the recuperation of the more critical patients.

Jack continued to irritate Peter by saying: "*The view outside is amazing. I can see a lovely garden and the sun is shining so brightly.*"

Infuriated with Jack's comment because he could not see the view for himself, Peter spat out: "*Will you just leave me in peace. I want to get some rest and you are getting on my nerves.*"

Jack was taken aback by the unprovoked comment but he

understood that his new friend must be feeling sorry for himself because of his state and so he didn't say another word as he wanted to respect his wishes.

The next day the sun again was shining and Peter awoke fearing that Jack would again make some comment about the lovely view that he could appreciate from his window view. However, much to Peter's surprise, there was silence. Also Jack was not in his bed. The bed was vacant. Moments later a nurse hurried into the room lifting the sheets from the vacant bed to change them. Peter was irritated. Why all this special attention to the newcomer? Now they were even changing his sheets? Peter's curiosity got the better of him and clearing his throat he asked the nurse: "Why such a fuss over that guy?"

The nurse glanced up at Peter and said softly: "*Jack passed away in his sleep last night. He suffered complications from the operation to remove the bullet to his lung that he received while trying to save an elderly woman from being assaulted in the street*". "By the way", the nurse added. *Last night I found a note near Jack's bedside. I believe that it is for you.*"

In awe and confusion Peter reached out for the note. On it was written: *Dear Peter, thank you for your company. I have a feeling that I do not have long now, however I hope that you continue to keep the faith as life is too short. Do not worry so much as to what is on the outside but rather focus on the joy that is within that you may share with others.*

In Faith, Jack ☺

Peter was taken aback. What did all this mean? He quickly asked the nurse to move him to the vacant bed where Jack had been. He needed to see for himself the view on the other side through the window. The nurse was obliging. She helped Peter onto the bed. Peter pushed himself up from the pillow to behold the beautiful view. Alas, his heart sank with disappointment. There was no view on the other side at all. There were only shutters concealing the view entirely. It then dawned on Peter that Jack had not been able to see any view on the outside, rather he was just trying to bring his own sunshine into the conversation.

Peter realised that he had made an error in judgement about Jack and that life has a way of teaching us valuable lessons, even when we are in denial at first.

James Allen said: "*Think lovingly, speak lovingly, act lovingly, and every need shall be supplied.*"

Therefore, aim to contribute to people's lives with joy and respect. Remember that first you must value yourself and be true to your inner child. Your inner self in its pure form is a child that wants to be loved and fulfilled. It needs time for growth and time to discover the beautiful world on the outside. This can only happen when we appreciate that the inner child is precious and it yearns for understanding and acceptance. If we are unable to accept the child within us, we will never be able to enjoy the beauty around us because we will always be at odds within ourselves. The outcome of this is that we will never be able to contribute at a grand and significant scale to the world because we will always sabotage our dreams by second-guessing them. When we embrace the child within, we simultaneously show the world that we have accepted who we are and the special role that we are to play in this lifetime.

Trusting that we have a divine purpose on this planet will lift us even in our darkest hours. With God everything is possible and those who believe that there is indeed a higher power than ourselves know that there is a reason behind all that happens to us and for us.

My friend I urge you to look within and to find what it is your purpose is. Do not rush your journey. Everything will happen in good time as it is supposed to. Through your experiences you will learn more about what it is you are destined to do and who it is you really are. You will contribute in a significant way to this world by being your authentic self and your authenticity will set you free from ordinary existence because you are aiming for your extraordinary self.

Dare to be your authentic self and shoot for the moon; you may end up in the stars if you miss but, then again, you know that you are a star in your own right.

Go ahead; create your dream, whatever it is. Be bold and honest with yourself and claim the destiny that is yours. A destiny filled with contribution, insight, love and difference. A destiny of wonder and creativity, where your spirit remains elevated and at peace, knowing that you played your part with deep meaning and significance while impacting the lives of others everlastingly.

For, as Victor Hugo said: *"There is nothing like a dream to create the future."*

Chapter Eight
The End (Omega)

"It seems to me we can never give up longing and wishing while we are thoroughly alive."

**George Eliot (Mary Ann Evans) (1819-1880)
(English novelist)**

As we reach the end of this book, I am comforted to know that in each ending there is always some new beginning. Life is cyclical, after all. Nothing really ends because life renews itself each and every day. Even when our spirit leaves our body and we take our last breath, life still continues. Maybe we are no longer physically present. Yet our spirit lives on.

The universe itself, as vast as it is, is small in comparison to the depth and size of the human spirit. Spirits defy gravity, time and space and are impossible to measure.

Spirits are infinite and endless.

Astronomers and astrologists often speak about the age of planets and stars and how many light years away from the earth they may be. The figures we have are as accurate as science and technology allow at any given point in time, however, who has ever measured the size of a single spirit? The answer to this question is – *no-one* and the reason for this is because it is impossible. There will never be an answer to this question because spirits are undefined by human beings.

If a spirit cannot be measured, then what is its potential? The answer to this question is infinite. The human potential is infinite and yet human beings live lives of mediocrity and complacency.

Humans beat themselves up when they believe that events end in some way. What humans fail to comprehend is that a new door opens to signify that we are closing another behind us. There are no endings it is just another stage of life that we are moving through. Life is full of different stages but it is all a part of the same masterpiece. Our journey began at birth and yet did it really begin there? Are we a piece in the larger puzzle of life? When we shut our eyes for the final time do we really end who we are? Are we the end of a new beginning?

The truth may be that we are neither the beginning nor the end of anything because if we take the idea that we were created, then the Alpha and the Omega (the beginning and the end) does not lie with us. We are not entirely in control of our destiny, so if this is the case, our destiny will unfold regardless. Our spirit is what defines us and yet from where has our spirit come from?

Whatever your individual beliefs may be, chances are you do not believe that you created yourself. If this is so, then you are a product of some divine creation and, if this is true for you, then you exist as a part of the whole. You are neither the beginning nor the end of the whole because, unlike a food chain where when one animal or plant is removed the others may perish, when humans depart from this earth, a power higher than ourselves ensures that life will continue for other humans. Spirits leave behind energy and this energy motivates us to continue on our path of greatness.

We must be all that we were destined to be. We need to breathe life into our dreams and work on ourselves constantly so as to live life to its fullest. We owe it to ourselves to play full out in order to leave our mark when our time is up. Remember there are no failures, only experiences and learning lessons that take us to a new page in our ultimate destiny.

In the words of Abraham Lincoln (1809-1865): "*I don't think much of a man who is not wiser today than he was yesterday.*"

So how will you better yourself today? Will you make time to live out your dreams or will you waste time on the side-lines watching other people live out their dreams?

Life is beautiful so embrace it and strive to be better than your best. You deserve it and no-one will give you the happiness or level of satisfaction that will complete you. Only you can complete yourself. Only you can be all that you were destined to be. Claim your right to greatness. Claim the extraordinary life that is yours!

Imagine your eternal power when you leave behind something of you even when you pass from this earth. Imagine leaving behind a screen-play, an art work, a book that you published, a charity that you contributed to or a scholarship that you funded. Imagine composing a song or setting up a fund for a child that you sponsored. Imagine creating a difference beyond time and space. Imagine being alive through the gifts of creation that you leave behind. Just imagine how powerful you can be and how powerful you really are NOW! Anything is possible if you believe; all you need is the belief to begin with.

When will you begin to create? When will you begin to be self-aware?

Will you leave your dreams until the end when you are possibly ill and frail?

Will you take a leap of faith and begin to work your magic NOW?

Will you understand that you are unrepeatable and irreplaceable in this life-time?

Will you make a stand to make a difference?

Will you live each day thankful for your blessings?

At this stage, let me give you an example of a very wealthy man that I knew. Allow me to call this man Samuel. Samuel migrated to Australia from Greece. He married, worked hard and had two sons. He built his own business that employed countless workers. His hard work began to pay off over the long years and he acquired great wealth. He subsequently gave to charities and organisations. Having worked hard, he retired and left the business in the hands of his sons to tend to and continue to see grow and prosper.

A few years ago, Samuel was diagnosed with cancer. Late last year, in his early seventies, Samuel was hospitalised and, shortly after, lost his battle. He went peacefully though. His funeral overflowed with people. He had left behind so much and had fulfilled his mission to his family, friends and society. He had created his legacy. His values and work ethic, applied on a daily basis, ensured that for many generations to come his family would be tended to and financially rewarded. His example of devotion, self-belief and perseverance are examples of an elevated spirit. A spirit that pushed on despite the obstacles and daily challenges.

It is the spirit of the warrior that we need to emulate. A warrior never gives in before combat. A warrior always looks for opportunities to grow and learn. Warriors love challenges because warriors know that it is through challenges that the greatest learning is experienced. Warriors have an eye for detail. They are focused and disciplined. Warriors study their competition and turn up prepared from their hours of training and self-study.

The truth is, until we study ourselves and work on our own

shortcomings, we will never be able to out perform our own expectations. When we are our own best coach, nothing or no-one will be able to hinder our purpose or make us live our life at any level other than at peak state.

Living with hope and conviction is imperative if we are to accomplish everything and anything we set our heart and mind to.

We need to re-ignite the spark in our life and to maintain the twinkle in our eye. Rub your hands together very, very quickly backwards and forwards. Create heat between your hands. After doing this for about sixty seconds, pull your hands away from each other. Do you feel a magnetic pull? The same thing happens in life; whatever we focus on we energise. The heat of our focus works like a magnet, attracting all the things we desire to come our way.

I urge you to live an energised and magnetic life. By putting out to the universe your desires and dreams, you create the energy for opportunities to come your way.

Believe in your magnetic potential. You are capable of greatness and of attracting great abundance in your life. By staying true to your dreams, you state to the universe that you will do whatever it takes to live an extraordinary life and chances are that the universe will stop what it is doing and hear your voice of passion and conviction.

Trust in your inner voice. Your inner voice is your guide, urging you to move forward to believe in yourself and your ultimate destiny. Each time you deny listening to your own voice, you choose to go against Spirit and Spirit wants what is best for you.

We see that people who are suffering from illness or disease and engage in negative self-talk disempower themselves and cut their own lives short.

The point is, how do you wish to be remembered? What is the meaning that you wish to attach to your life? What do you stand for? What are your visions and motivations in life?

What is your alpha and what is your omega? In other words, what will you choose to live for or even die for?

What do you want to be remembered for? Who will you love, inspire and believe in? Who will you make laugh? Who will you motivate? Which lives will you touch? How will this world have been a better place because you passed by?

I guess we are all trying to find a meaning in this life. A reason for being and a reason for continuing on our quest. What is your reason?

In life, there are never real endings. Each day is a new beginning. I even have a beautiful portrait of a sunrise at home in my bedroom and underneath it reads: "**OPPORTUNITY – Each day is a new beginning**".

I bought this portrait many years ago at a time when I was not feeling the best, both physically and emotionally. I was running on low energy and spiritual fuel and, subconsciously, I was looking for something of inspiration. When I saw this dazzling portrait of the sunrise, I knew that this image of the sunrise had been waiting for me. It was the perfect phrase to capture what I was seeking to create and that was the acceptance of each day and the ability to create thoughts and experiences each and every day of life. We can choose to see everything as an opportunity to learn or grow from, rather than as a set back that we beat ourselves over. We can let each day that passes go and bless it because we know that the day that departs has taught us more about ourselves and our quest for meaning in this life. We can then appreciate that the new day that comes should be welcomed and appreciated. Remember whatever we appreciate, appreciates and whatever we doubt, diminishes.

Albert Einstein once said: *"There are two ways to live your life. One is as though nothing is a miracle. The other is as though everything is a miracle."*

Whether you are a spiritual person or not or believe in "miracles", what is important is that you believe in blessings. Surely, it is a blessing to be alive, to live in a democracy, to have freedom of speech, religion and movement. Think about places in the world where people do not enjoy these basic rights.

Amnesty International send me their regular magazine that includes articles, accounts and pictures of people who have been tortured/imprisoned or reprimanded in the countries that they live in. For example, a person in country X, may have been shot or beaten to death for taking part in a demonstration or rally.

Just think for a moment how blessed you truly are!

Life is a beautiful adventure and gratitude is required. Without gratitude all we do loses its meaning. When we are ungrateful, we send out a message to the Universe that says that we do not appreciate all the good things that are coming our way. The Universe may just react to our attitude and decide to take from us what we have been ungrateful for and give it to someone else who will be appreciative instead.

Remember to thank the Universe for the gifts bestowed upon you today. The Universe may just decide to reward you and give you much more of what you want and ask for…

Live the life that you always imagined. Think about what you want to attract each and every day. Work towards your goals with thirst and vigour. Be thankful for your gifts and talents. Appreciate the people around you who have believed in you and who have helped you on your path. Trust in your Spirit. Know that each day is indeed a new beginning and that you have all the resources available to you to create your divine destiny.

Have faith that all will go well. Pace yourself with humility and be gentle with yourself. Remember you are a child of this Universe and you can make a difference in your life and the lives of those around you, should you choose to. Everything in this life is a matter of choice and we all have the ability to choose our path.

Remember to smile often and to keep a positive outlook. As George Asaf, the American songwriter exclaimed: "*What's the use of worrying? It never was worthwhile, so pack up your troubles in your old kit-bag, and smile, smile, smile.*"

Life happens to us because of our convictions and behaviours.

All we do and say has some form of result. Even inaction is a decision. A troubled mind and heart lead to haphazard results. Trust in your inner voice and intuition. Keep on going. Refrain from looking backwards. Only do so when you are trying to take a lesson from the past. History is there to teach us but the NOW demands to be lived and enjoyed. The future will be the result of your hard work and contribution in the present.

Know that you are destined for greatness. Know that there is something that you were brought to this planet to work towards/give/invent/create. Discover what it is that you were destined to become. Knowing yourself is above all the most important lesson to learn.

Imagine that you were a prime-minister or a president for a day. What would you do? Who would you meet? What would you attend to? Where would you go?

I hear you ask: "But is a single day enough?" The answer to the question is every moment counts. Lives can be changed not only in a day but in seconds. Think about a world athlete who has just broken a world record by seconds. Think about a bomb that can go off in seconds. Think about a loved one that you may lose in a second. Think about falling asleep at the wheel for a second.

The truth is our lives may change in a second. You do not need to be a prime-minister or a president to change people's lives; you may decide to create a difference in a second. You may choose to be a person of influence in your field, in your community, in your church, in your family, in your relationship. You may choose to uplift yourself and others, wherever you are. You may lead by example and help others realise their dreams too.

You are a beacon of light and your Spirit yearns to live out its dreams of creativity. Dare to shine! Dare to allow your inspiration and insight to lead the way.

Dare to experience your own enlightenment.

Be the best that you can be because anything less is compromise.

Napoleon Hill once said: ... "*Look not to the things that are seen but to the things that are unseen, for the things that are seen are transient, the things that are unseen are eternal.*"

Know that life is a continual series of experiences and that you must venture within in order to understand what your purpose is supposed to be. Yes, sometimes life may not bring us the things we hoped for but, then again, life always has a way of bringing what we are ready for our way. Even when we believe that we are unready to handle life's blows, we ultimately get resourceful and surprise ourselves by getting through what we believed at first would be an unconquerable "storm".

Positive self-talk is imperative at times of unease and distress. Denis Waitley once said: "*The most important conversations you'll ever have are the conversations you will have with yourself.*"

It is also important to action what we wish to create in our lives. As Thomas Henry Huxley suggests: "*The great end in life is not knowledge but action.*"

Therefore, believe that your life is a continual process of growth, achievement and learning. Know that there is a reason why you are on this planet and your mission ought to be to find out what it is you were destined to do, be or create.

Your life is not an accident. Nothing on this planet happens by chance. Everything is happening for a reason and for you to evolve into a more capable, self-motivated and enlightened human being.

Eleanor Roosevelt (1884-1962) who had been a First Lady of the United States, a writer and diplomat, had this to say about character building: *"Character-building begins in our infancy and continues until death."*

Life is about constant evolution and learning. We are born not knowing much more than that we require love, food, rest and shelter to survive, however, over the years through education, training, parental and social support, we develop our sense of personality and ideas about who we are and what we want out of life.

We learn that life is indeed to be enjoyed and lived. We all long to experience elation in our romantic relationships and to find a meaning in what it is we are doing for a living. The challenge is that most people do not enjoy what they do and so cannot find the meaning in their every day actions. When we are not passionate about where we are spending most of our time, we lose touch of our direction or purpose. This sense of meaninglessness eats away at our soul, very much like termites eat away at wood.

The challenge is to discover what it is you are passionate about and what brings both peace and joy to your soul. Continue doing whatever it is that lifts your Spirit. Deep down, you know that Spirit cannot be denied for too long.

Dare to get out of your comfort zone! Dare to venture out and experience the world of uncharted waters that you wish to travel to. Dare to climb the Everest of your wildest dreams. Dare to aim for the summit of your ultimate destiny!

Strangely enough, we all know that from the moment we are born we are also dying. Therefore, we do not know when it is that we will take our last breath. Live each day like it is your last. Honour your time instead of "killing time" like so many people refer to.

If today was indeed your last day, what is it that you would do, say, create? Who would you want to thank, forgive or hug?

Remember that forgiveness unbinds us from past grievances. Holding onto past memories, hurts, upsets or events only inhibits our NOW! So let go of what was in order to embrace the present moment which is the door to the future.

The English poet Alexander Pope (1688-1744) had this to say about forgiveness:

"To err is human, to forgive, divine."

Another beautiful quote on forgiveness is the following by the psychiatrist and writer M. Scott Peck:

"The reason to forgive is for your own sake. For our own health. Because beyond that point needed for healing, if we hold onto our anger, we stop growing and our souls begin to shrivel."

Therefore, let go of your past grievances. Everything happened as it did to teach you lessons. Lessons that made you stronger, wiser and more equipped to deal with the present. You have come a long way on your journey of personal development and you have many accomplishments to be proud of. You have done the best that you could have done with the knowledge that you had available at the time and so now the moment has come to let go of it all and to forge forward with ease and speed into your future.

You deserve a wonderful future and so go now confidently in the direction of your dreams and experience, learn and create all that you were destined to!

Know that you will only cheat yourself of your magical destiny if you refuse to embrace the NOW and stubbornly hold onto the past. The past is over. It happened and left. The decision is yours whether you want to live in a past dead life or in the NOW that is urging you to make a change, to make decisions for your brilliant tomorrow.

Let me give you an example of a young man who I knew about. Allow me to call him Mark. Mark was a bright and talented young man with a great thirst to succeed financially in life. He worked in a prestigious law firm and had the lifestyle that most would admire.

However, in reality, Mark had no balance in his life. He worked incredibly long hours, even going to work on weekends. He had no relationship and he was getting old before his time. His deep and burning question was: *What is this all about? Am I truly happy?*

Mark was unhappy, as we can all comprehend. Maybe what appears to make us happy on the outside is not necessarily what makes us happy on the inside.

True happiness comes from the inside first. It does not work the other way around!

We cannot deny our feelings. Because feelings indicate what is going on inside us. How many times have we had that gut feeling about something and yet proceeded to deny that feeling, only to discover soon after that we went against our inner wisdom?

Humans are indeed beautiful and unique. They are complex and yet wish for the simple things, like love and significance.

The truth is many people have survived without much money but few people can survive without love. A life devoid of love can be quite lonely and isolating. There is indeed no greater power on this earth than to love and to be loved in return.

Mother Teresa had this to say about love: *"Let us not be satisfied with just giving money. Money is not enough, money can be got, but they need your hearts to love them. So, spread love everywhere you go: first of all in your own home. Give love to your children, to your wife or husband, to a next-door neighbour."*

Know that love empowers people to action. Love can make that long day appear much more acceptable because we know that we have someone other than ourselves to care for.

Love can make us lighter on our feet because we are lifted by a higher purpose to share our thoughts, our feelings and our dreams with someone else who understands our essence.

Life without love is like food without good wine. As humans, we search for self-truth and then we yearn to find someone to share our truth with. True love is, therefore, a combination of spiritual, mental, emotional and physical bonding.

Therefore, love who you are and seek a person to share your unique love with. Someone who will understand you when others misunderstand and someone who wishes to see you grow and be the best that you can be.

Do not underestimate the power of your heart and emotions. The Chinese philosopher, Confucius, said:

> "To put the world in order we must first put the nation in order;
>
> To put the nation in order, we must first put the family in order;
>
> To put the family in order, we must cultivate our personal life;
>
> And to cultivate our personal life, we must set our hearts right."

Once again, in regard to the power of the heart, the French novelist and aviator Antoine de Saint-Exupery had this to say:

> "And now here is my secret, a very simple secret; it is only with the heart that one can see properly; what is essential is invisible to the eye."

So take some time out today to examine what you are feeling about the state of your life and heart. What is lifting you? What is causing you worry or unease?

Go in the direction of your joy. Pursue your heart's passions and fear not what others think or say. People are all entitled to their opinions, but the opinion that counts the most is your own!

Reach out for all the good things that you deserve. Learn to discern what enriches your soul and where you should be investing your energy and time.

Decide that your life will be unique and marvellous. Choose to forgive, let go of and accept what was. Choose to love your life and the people who share your special moments on your journey.

Remember there are no true endings. Everything is a cycle and we live on, even when our Spirit leaves our body. We live on through the memories we created in others and through the legacy we will leave behind.

Live by example. Your example may affect the generations to come and so you have a responsibility not only to yourself but to the universe to be the best that you can be!

Think of the life of Jesus Christ and to the significant spread of Christianity today. Think about the incredible legacy that was created and how the actions of Jesus and His leading by example affected humanity forevermore.

Dear reader, as I now draw to the close of my final chapter THE END (OMEGA), I want you to know that this is just the start for you. Remember there are no true endings after all as we have discussed. This is your beginning. This is your ALPHA. Each day is a new blessing with new gifts to offer. Embrace the moment and your greatness.

Most of all, as an anonymous writer once wrote: "*Don't cry because it's over, smile because it happened.*"

Smile because you deserve to. Smile because each day you can make choices and decisions to propel you in the direction of your destiny.

Smile because you have been blessed with rare qualities and talents unlike anyone else. You are irreplaceable and unrepeatable. There never was and there will never be another you. There is just one you and so you owe it to yourself to shine!

It has been an honour sharing my thoughts with you on my own journey through this book. I have enjoyed each moment of creation and growth and having the opportunity to share these ideas with you. It is my faith that each of you will take what it is you require from these pages to continue on your own personal quest for meaning and purpose in your life.

I thank you for investing your time to assist yourself in your enlightenment and self-awareness.

Continue to be you. You are beautiful and capable in every way. Claim your destiny and your right to be happy and fulfilled.

Allow me to fill a glass to you and to toast to your brilliant success in everything you do.

This is your life and this is, after all, the beginning…

BIBLIOGRAPHY

- Eckhart Tolle: "*The Power of Now*" (Hachette Live Australia Pty Ltd., © 2004, Australia)

- "*Holy Bible*" (Thomas Nelson Inc, © 1970, United States of America)

- Paulo Coelho: "The Alchemist" (Harper Perennial edition, © 1998, United States of America)

- Rhonda Byrne: "*The Secret*" (TS Production Limited Liability Co, © 2004, China)

- Stephanie Giannis: "*Envision the Vision...You!*" (Hippo Books, 2003, Sydney, Australia)

- Stephanie Giannis: "*Fragments of Truth*" (Library of Congress, © 2002, United States of America)

- Victor E. Frankl: "*Man's Search for Meaning*" (Washington Square Press, ©1984, United States of America)

NEW RELEASES... ALSO FROM SID HARTA PUBLISHERS

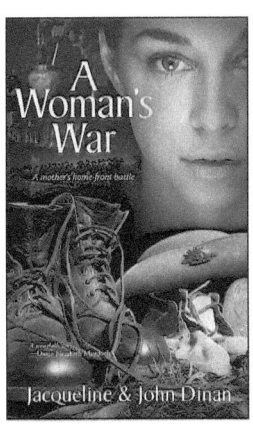

OTHER BEST SELLING SID HARTA TITLES CAN BE FOUND AT
http://sidharta.com.au   http://Anzac.sidharta.com
***

HAVE YOU WRITTEN A STORY?
http://publisher-guidelines.com

NEW RELEASES... ALSO FROM SID HARTA PUBLISHERS

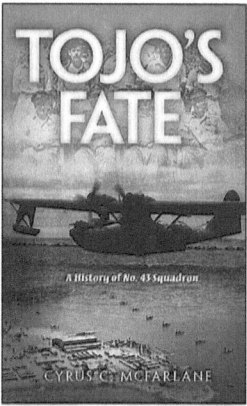

OTHER BEST SELLING SID HARTA TITLES CAN BE FOUND AT
http://sidharta.com.au   http://Anzac.sidharta.com
❉❉❉
HAVE YOU WRITTEN A STORY?
http://publisher-guidelines.com

Best-selling titles by Kerry B. Collison

Readers are invited to visit our publishing websites at:
http://sidharta.com.au
http://publisher-guidelines.com/

Kerry B. Collison's home pages:
http://www.authorsden.com/visit/author.asp?AuthorID=2239
http://www.expat.or.id/sponsors/collison.html
email: author@sidharta.com.au

Purchase Sid Harta titles online at:
http://sidharta.com.au

NEW RELEASES... ALSO FROM SID HARTA PUBLISHERS

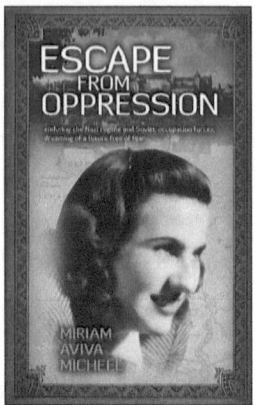

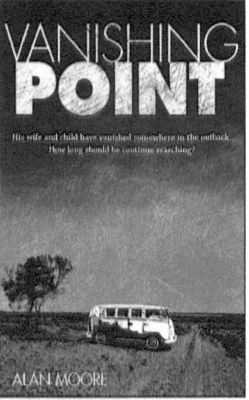

OTHER BEST SELLING SID HARTA TITLES CAN BE FOUND AT
http://sidharta.com.au   http://Anzac.sidharta.com

HAVE YOU WRITTEN A STORY?
http://publisher-guidelines.com